Contemporary
FURNITURE

A. F. BICK Teacher, Public Schools, Milwaukee, Wis., and Milwaukee Downer College. Formerly teacher of design and methods, Colorado College of A. & M., summer; Kent State University, summer; University of Wisconsin, Extension Division.

THE BRUCE PUBLISHING COMPANY
MILWAUKEE

Library of Congress Catalog Card Number: 54–7782

(2/60)

Introduction

CONTEMPORARY FURNITURE, the title of this book, suggests a new and open style such as a highly scientific and industrial age might be expected to design.

At the beginning of our century, fortunately for us, a few experimenters, architects, engineers, and industrial designers actively resisted the stagnation of "period" design, and injected into the indifference and complacency of the age concepts of recreation. Their new forms were called *contemporary*. Their buildings took on a quality of light and spaciousness and their furniture became light in weight and color, simple, and pleasing to the eye. Their tables, cabinets, and chairs may be said to express, as well as wood may, "space and time."

The question, then, is: What shall a teacher or a craftsman do about *contemporary* furniture? The answer is obvious. Contemporary furniture, architecture, and fabrics are facts in everyday life. If he accepts them and understands them, well and good. If not, he must consider that they constitute an area of thought which he must be ready and able to evaluate in relation to other values of his age, and to interpret the new forms to his students. This may require the elimination of previously held prejudices in order to arrive at unbiased and thoughtful conclusions. Then he will look for teaching material such as that which this book is designed to supply.

There are within its covers a large variety of contemporary items that are easy to make. Some are simple school and home shop pieces which will be found useful by teachers, craftsmen, or therapists. Other projects which at first might appear very difficult are still within the capacity of those who have gained experience in working from drawings.

Contemporary design is spontaneous, clean, and new, and gives the impression of honesty and sincerity. The era for which it is a symbol is great in its own right as an age of strength, self-confidence, inventive ability, and engineering skill.

In wood, these qualities appear in the form of fitness of the material, lightness of structure and tone, simplicity of surface, excellence of line and proportion, and faultlessness of finish.

Bibliography

The following publications are suggested as excellent sources for the study of contemporary furniture and home design.

*Bibliography of Professional
Source Material*

The Magazine of Building, Time, Inc. (New York 20, N. Y., 9 Rockefeller Plaza, $6.00 annually)

Design Quarterly, Walker Art Center (Minneapolis 5, Minn., 1710 Lyndale Ave., South, $2.00 annually)

Interiors, Whitney Publications, Inc. (New York 22, N. Y., 18 East 50th St., $7.00 annually)

The current *Catalogue of Knoll Associates, Inc.*, 575 Madison Ave., New York 22, N. Y., $3.50 each

The current *Catalogue of Herman Miller Furniture Co.*, Zeeland, Mich., $5.00 each.

The names of many men and art museums stand out boldly today as the vanguard of the contemporary movement. These will become familiar through the recommended reading.

Contents

Chapter 1 Tool Processes

No attempt is made by the author of this book to discuss machine or hand tool procedures. The following paragraphs aim only to clarify a few of the special methods mentioned in the text.

1. The first is the matter of producing curves in heavy thicknesses of wood. Four possible processes are listed:

    The contour is cut roughly with crosscut and ripsaws. Then it is

    a) Trimmed to the line with the plane moving directly across the edge, the plane being held 75 deg. off the axis of movement, the front turned in the direction of the grain, see Figure 1,

    b) or it may be chiseled across from each side, paring down the grain, as in Figure 2.

    c) It may also be chiseled with the grain as in Figure 3, or

    d) it may be filed with rasp and cabinet file in the direction shown in Figure 4.

2. Concave curves in very heavy thicknesses may be cut by making backsaw kerfs across the edge at quarter-inch intervals. These are then broken

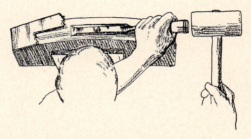

Fig. 3. Producing a curve by chiseling with the grain.

Fig. 1. Producing a curve using a plane.

Fig. 2. Producing a curve by paring with a chisel.

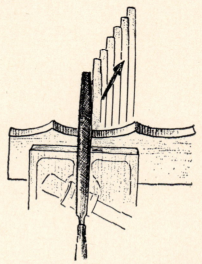

Fig. 4. Producing a curve with a file.

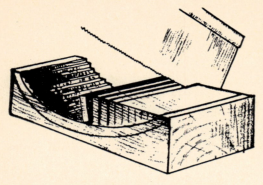

Fig. 5. Producing a concave curve.

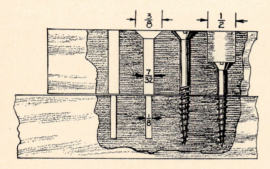

Fig. 6. Drilling for a No. 10 screw.

Fig. 7. Chiseling mortises.

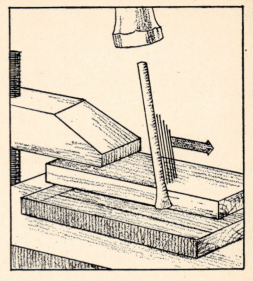

Fig. 8. Chasing decorative lines.

Fig. 9. Modeling cutout appliqué
ornament.

out and chiseled to the line, as in Figure 5.

3. Drilling and boring is done horizontally while the piece to be drilled is held in a vise or clamp. The head of the brace or hand drill is held against the body. This method is economical of bits and drills, and of energy, especially when boring into end grain.

How to drill for No. 10 screws is illustrated in Figure 6, the principle shown being fundamental for all screws and bolts.

4. Boring at fixed angles may be done with the help of a bevel square, but a jig made of a hardwood block bored to the proper angle is preferable for accuracy. One such simple jig is

Fig. 10. Appliqué ornament applied in place.

shown on the detail for Plate 1. The drill in the illustration is shown fitted with a wood depth gauge.

5. Mortises are rough chiseled as in Figure 7, and thereafter trimmed to knife and gauge lines by careful paring.

6. Decorative lines are chased or scraped along straight edges as in Figure 8, the scraping being done with the sharpened edge of a screw driver or file.

7. Cut out appliqué ornaments, similar to the type shown in Figure 9, are modeled by filing after they are fastened with glue to a carving board. When the ornament is finished, it is cut or soaked off the board, and applied with glue to its final background as shown in Figure 10.

8. Chamfering end grain is illustrated in Figure 11.

Fig. 11. Chamfering end grain.

Chapter 2 The Method of Starting a Job

The approach, it is said, is half the job. Standard hand-tool and machine procedures vary with every job. It is an economy to plan each particular problem so that work may follow a logical sequence. The aim should be to approach each job with ease and with economy of time and material.

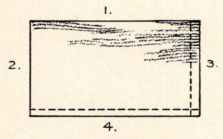

Fig. 12. Cutting out stock.

1. Where only one piece of wood is to be made, the order of procedure is as illustrated in Figure 12. Plane sides 1 and 2 (working edge and working end), then measure off the length and, lastly, the width. Then cut and plane to lines.
2. Where a variety of small pieces are to be made, the basic hand approach is to work with stock just large enough to include all small pieces together. Where pieces vary in length and width, as in making the box shown in Figure 10, where six small pieces are used, it is not a matter of cutting out wood for each separate part singly, but of working out as many of them as possible out of a larger piece. Therefore, refer to Figure 13, where the steps of procedure are numbered:

a) Plane straight edge (called *working edge*).
b) Plane one end square (the *working end*).
c) Gauge the width of top and bottom board all along the stock, and plane to the gauge line. Notice that side and end pieces are also planed in the third operation. It is logical therefore that they remain on the parent board until everything is done that may be done before separating them.
d) Measure length of top, draw line, saw, and plane to line.
e) Plane new square end.
f) Measure length of bottom piece, draw line, saw, and plane to line. Notice now that the ends of the remaining piece are not to be planed at this time.
g) Gauge widths of sides and ends from both planed edges of remaining piece.
h) Rip, and plane to lines. Even now, the pieces remain intact until all that is possible is done while they are in one piece.

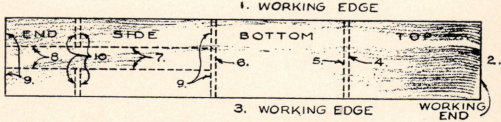

Fig. 13. Cutting pieces out of a larger piece of lumber.

i) Plane the two ends of both pieces. If you have a metal miter box, the ends may be sawed square instead. If planed, the process shown in Figure 14 is the simplest for short ends: the piece is held against the back block of a bench hook and the plane operated on its side, as shown. A slightly heavier shaving than usual may be removed.

Fig. 14. Using the bench hook for planing short ends.

j) Lay out the lengths of sides and

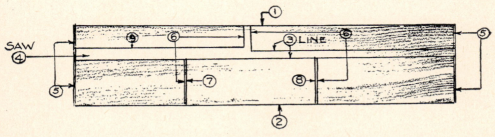

Fig. 15. Grouping pieces of like dimensions before cutting.

ends, draw lines, and cut with backsaw. Plane to lines, or cut the pieces against a gauge in a miter box.

This and similar procedures are used throughout the book. Remember to use the basic principle, just described, whenever possible.

3. As a third example of procedure, it may be well to consider the many instances where there are unequal lengths and widths that may be grouped conveniently with pieces of the same width, running the length of the board. Look through the list of pieces to be made, and segregate like dimensions, pairing groups of approximate length, as illustrated in Figure 15.

The procedure is:

a) Plane straight edge.

b) Plane parallel side, regardless of width of stock.

c) Gauge widths of narrow boards,

and measure widths of wide boards and draw lines.

d) Rip, and plane to lines.

e) Plane square, both ends of each board.

f) Measure lengths from each squared end, crosscut, and plane all to lines.

If all pieces are of equal widths, the process is the same.

4. The fourth example is that of cutting multiple pieces, more than two in the width of the board and one or more in the length. The logical procedure is illustrated in Figure 16.

If students are not given proper directions, they invariably mark off all their pieces at once and saw between lines. This is not as successful as the given approach:

a and *b*) Plane both edges of stock, regardless of the sizes to be made.

c) Gauge lines from both planed edges to the width of both pieces

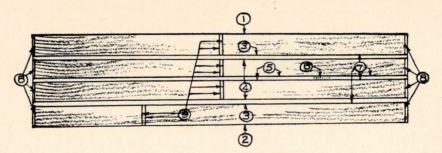

Fig. 16. Cutting multiple pieces.

or groups to be cut. Rip, and plane to lines.

d) Replane both edges on remaining piece.

e) Gauge lines for next pieces, working from both sides of stock.

f) Rip, and plane to lines.

g) Continue this if there are more strips to be made.

h) After all ripping and planing to gauged lines has been done, plane all the ends of the strips that contain more than one piece. Plane but one end of strips that contain but one length.

i) Measure all lengths, draw lines, saw and plane to lines, using the process illustrated in Figure 14, or cut against the gauge in a miter box.

The procedure just outlined, applies whether the boards to be cut have the same or different widths. For instance, one strip may be 2 in. wide, the second 7 in., and the third 1½ in. The process is the same for all.

5. Machine procedures follow somewhat the same plan.

   a) From the list of parts to be made, separate those of equal width and equal thickness. These are cut out of a long piece at a saving of time, first in widths, and then in lengths as given. It is always best to cut all pieces of a particular machine setting at one running.

b) If it is necessary to cut several pieces of the same length, or of like or unlike width, the machine is set with a stop against and from which pieces may be gauged to make all alike.

c) The procedure in machine sawing is like that of handsawing in that the first step is always the cutting of the base straight edge. The second step may vary, the machine always cutting the sides parallel to each other. Cutting to length follows.

d) If the board is to be used for parts of different widths the practice is to cut the stock into pieces each of which includes but one width. Edge truing is easier on stock not too long.

e) After the foregoing has been taken care of, square one end of each piece, measure off the lengths, and cut the pieces to size. No attempt will be made here to describe hand or machine operations.

6. Making round legs by hand. All rounded parts proceed from the square form, through octagonal and sixteen sides to the round. For example, the tables in Plates 29, 30, and 31, required tapered round legs. The procedure is: Draw compass circles of the required size on each end of the stock and plane down to these circles, proceeding from the square through

the octagonal, then to a sixteen-sided polygon, and finally to the round. Orderly procedure insures uniformity of the product and cuts down the time. Then sand the legs round. Hold the post in the hand, the most of it on the bench, the hand hooked over the edge, and rotate the piece slowly while sanding back and forth with No. ½ garnet paper held on a block. The slow, regular rotation will result in perfect rounding.

7. Cutting the tenon or dowel on the top of round legs. When legs fit into sockets as they do on tables, shown in Plates 27, 30, 31, and 38, the rounded legs are set, one by one, vertically into the vise, protected against marring by the vise jaws with a wrapping of paper or cloth. Mark the dowel size with a compass on the top face, and cut vertically down with backsaw on each side and close to the compass mark, first in the square and then the octagonal. Follow this with a rasp until the dowels are round. Next, fit the dowel into its socket, mark the shoulder, scribing the line parallel to the underside of the table, and then saw the shoulder. Split the dowel halfway down with a backsaw, glue the leg into the socket, and drive an oak or maple wedge into the split with glue. Lastly, trim off the top with a saw, protecting the table with a piece of cardboard. Then smooth off the top with sandpaper.

Chapter 3 Assembly Procedures

1. The first procedure in constructing a piece of furniture is to plane the surfaces of all component parts, reducing the thickness as little as possible. Usually sanding follows, but no joining edges or ends should be sanded. In fact, open edges and ends are left for postassembly finishing in most cases.

2. Before nailing top or bottom, true the level of previous assembly, holding plane on adjacent sides to insure level planing, as in Figure 17.

Fig. 17. Planing a top edge level.

3. Nails and screws are placed where they will hold to the best advantage, i.e., reasonably near the ends, but far enough away not to weaken the wood grain. Basswood takes nails well with a minimum of splitting. It is therefore favored for small projects. Basswood is not drilled for nails except in instances where the job compels nailing close to the edge. In such cases, and where nails are to be driven into brittle and hard woods, holes are drilled prior to nailing. As an economy, such holes may be drilled with headless nails of the size used as bits. Usually holes are drilled through the top piece to be nailed, and not through the second.

4. All screw holes in furniture are drilled and countersunk. The procedure, for a No. 10 by 1½-in. screw, for example, is illustrated in Figure 6.

   The upper hole must be snug to loose, not tight. The lower hole should be equal to the core diameter of the screw, or less, depending on the hardness of wood. If the screw is to be hidden, counterbore instead of countersink, and fill the counter with a wood plug. If the available screws are short in length, counterbore and set them deeper.

5. Glue joints without reinforcement are used where there are no strains. Otherwise, tongue and groove, and dowel joints with glue are standard. Front strips may be fastened with nails and glue, and where added strength in a joint is required, because of strains due to heavy service, glue is used with screws. Wipe surplus glue off the job immediately, and wash off outer areas to save tedious sanding.

   Glue types have changed materially in recent years. The best now may be superseded tomorrow. Today, *Woodlok* is an excellent, white, ready-to-use cold liquid glue that does not discolor the joint. Casein and resin glues are very good, and Franklin liquid animal glue is tough and flexible. These and possibly others are readily recommended.

6. The principle in cabinetwork is to build beautifully grained, light, strong structures with hidden joints, none of the means of joining being visible to the eye. The most useful of the hidden joints are the mortise and tenon,

the cross lap, the dovetail, and the dowel. In this book the use of dowel joints is recommended. The advantage of the dowel joint is its simplicity. It easily increases the glue area, thereby adding strength to the joint. Use ⅜-in. dowels for 1-in. wood, ⁵⁄₁₆-in. for ½-in. wood, ¼-in. for ⅜-in. wood, etc.

a pile, mark all ends from the front face. Make a corresponding line on two inner faces of the legs, moving the gauge down the outside faces. This marks the distance for the dowel to be set into the wood from the front.

e) Using the same measurement on the gauge, mark down from the

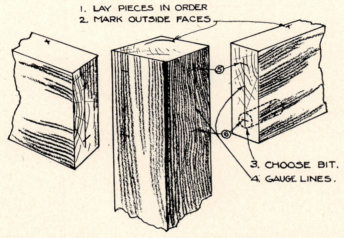

Fig. 18. Laying out the position for the dowel holes.

A table leg joint is made as follows:

a) Examine the grain of the parts to be assembled, placing the favored sides toward the front. Lay parts in order.

b) Mark preferred tops and outsides.

c) Mark position of dowel holes to be bored. In a table like the one in Plate 41, item A, where legs are 1⅜ in. square, and rails 1 by 1⅝ in. on the end face, dowels are placed as close to the upper and lower edges as the wood strength allows, for it is at these points that the major strains are located. The writer can give no further rule for the positioning of holes. His best judgment places them ⅜ in. from each edge.

d) Set the marking gauge at ⅜ in., and placing the group of rails in

top side of the ends, crossing the first line. Do the same on all legs.

f) Now set the gauge at 1¼ in., and repeat the same marking. There should then be two marked positions for holes on each joining surface. See Figure 18.

g) Bore each ⅜-in. hole 1 in. deep, placing the rails into the vise as a stack and boring horizontally. Place the legs into the vise vertically and bore them in the same way.

h) Cut dowels ¼ in. shorter than total hole measurement.

i) Put glue in all holes, on all dowels, and on both joint faces, assemble and clamp, Figure 19. The first clamps grip the sides of the joint, drawing the ends tight. The second set grip over the first set

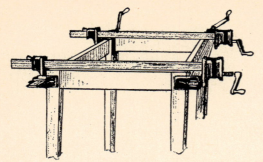

Fig. 19. Clamping a table-leg
assembly.

and over the top of the table assembly, drawing the edges of the
clamp bars toward the joint and
drawing the sides tight. The area
under the pressure of the bar is
protected by a strip of wood.

j) Check the table. If it is not square,
correct the discrepancy by cross
clamping.

Table legs sometimes appar-
ently stop below rails. Actually,

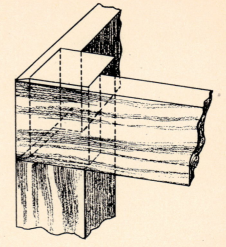

Fig. 20. One method of assembling
table rails and legs.

they continue behind the cutout
rail to the top, being doweled as
before. The rail is mitered at the
corners. See Figure 20 and Table *C* on Plate 41.

Chapter 4 Steps in Finishing

The term *finishing* includes all steps to and including the final wax polishing. Each must be completed in order. The following lists all of these steps.

1. Plane all surfaces, if that has not already been done.
2. Final all-over smoothing of parts to make them part of the structure. This may include the removal of sharp edges and corners, and the correction of curves from one piece into another.
3. Filling all nail holes and faults with a mixture of glue and sandpaper dust, unless the crack is too open, when it is filled with matched wood. These fillings are sanded when still damp.
4. Final all-over sanding in the following steps.
   a) Sand all over with No. ½ garnet paper, held on a sanding block.
   b) Then sand with No. 2-0, and, last,
   c) With No. 6–0 garnet paper, each grade taking off the marks of the preceding sanding, until all surfaces are smooth.
5. Cover the job all over with boiled linseed oil, unless otherwise specified. Substitute three coats of clear lacquer where the lightest shade of wood color is desired.

   These coatings fill the grain, harden the surface, and bring out the grain figure. They are water and scratch proof. Boiled oil may be applied with cloth. This is an old, much used finish, and an excellent and proved base for the finish coats that may follow. Allow two or three days or a week to harden. Then rub to glass smoothness with worn sandpaper of fine grade.
6. The overcoating may be wax, varnish, or paint.
   a) If a wax finish is wanted, apply it generously, using a car-type paste wax. Allow an hour or more to set, after which rub to a polish. Repeat the next day, and the next. The time interval is worth considering. Applying a second coat on semihard wax removes much of the first coat. The last hard rubbing should produce a beautifully finished job.
   b) Varnish should be applied with a dustless brush in a dust-free room on a dustless surface. Apply the coats just thin enough not to run, and cover the surface evenly. Allow about two days for drying, then rub down smooth with fine wet sandpaper. Wipe off the dust with a damp cloth, and repeat the coating and rubbing. After the third coat, rub with 3/0 or 4/0 steel wool until the work is down to a uniform satin finish all over — edges, corners, and all.

Chapter 5 Projects

The making of boxes is a fundamental woodworking problem. The method should be logical, practical, and economical of time and material and the principles involved should be applied in making many of the other pieces described in this book.

Box No. 1 — Figures 21, 22, and 23

Material: Basswood
Stock size: $\frac{3}{8} \times 5\frac{1}{2} \times 30$
Finish: Natural, in oil and wax

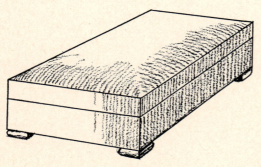

Fig. 21. Box No. 1.

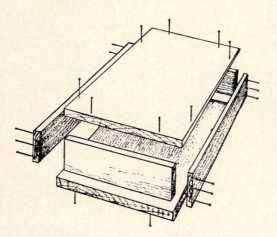

Fig. 22. Nailing box together.

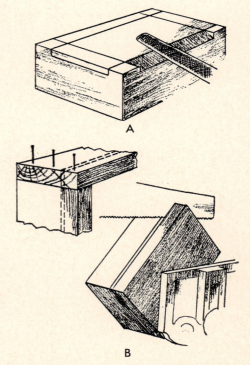

Fig. 23. A, cutting the feet for boxes Nos. 5 and 7; B, separating the cover from the box.

PROCEDURE

1. Using the method given in Chapter 2, cut out the following pieces:
   Top, 1 pc. $\frac{3}{8} \times 5 \times 8$
   Bottom, 1 pc. $\frac{3}{8} \times 5 \times 8$
   Sides, 2 pcs. $\frac{3}{8} \times 1\frac{1}{4} \times 8$
   Ends, 2 pcs. $\frac{3}{8} \times 1\frac{1}{4} \times 4\frac{1}{4}$
2. Plane all pieces and sand inside surfaces.
3. Nail sides to ends, using three No. 16 by 1-in. brads. See Figure 22.
4. True up the top and bottom of the box, and then nail the top to one edge. After aligning the body with the top, fasten the remainder in place with No. $18 \times \frac{3}{4}$-in. wire brads.

5. For feet, draw pencil lines around the bottom, sides, and ends, ¾ and ¼ in. respectively, A, Figure 23, and cut to lines. Then finish with a wood rasp as shown.

6. To separate the cover from the box, set a marking gauge at ¾ in., and again at ⅞ in., draw lines around the box, as shown in Figure 23, and rip between the lines. After proceeding down far enough to admit the point of the ripsaw inside the box, follow the single pair of lines all around. However, before cutting the last side, insert something of kerf thickness into the opposite end of the cut to prevent splitting.

7. Plane both sawed edges to lines, as illustrated in Chapter 3.

8. Round the top, drawing a ¼-in. line around the sides and ends and a 1¼-in. line over the top all around. Set top nails deep and chamfer to lines. For end chamfering, use the plane as in Figure 11. The upper arrises are now planed and rounded as illustrated.

9. Place the box, closed, into the vise and sand all around. Set the hinges and finish as directed in Chapter 4.

Box No. 2 — Figure 24

Use the same basic procedure outlined for box No. 1, changing the over-all dimensions to 2 by 4 by 6 in. The sizes of parts to be made are:

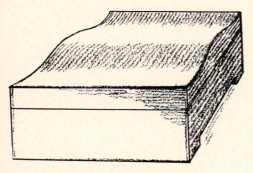

Fig. 24. Box No. 2.

2 pcs. ⅜ × 4 × 6, top and bottom
2 pcs. ⅜ × 1¼ × 6, sides
2 pcs. ⅜ × 1¼ × 3¼, ends

Curve the top to a depth of ¼ in., using the method for producing curves in heavy thicknesses of wood in Chapter 1. Feet are filed as in Figure 13.

Box No. 3 — Figure 25

The dimensions of the box in Figure 25 are 5 by 4¾ by 5½ in. The sizes of parts to be made are:

2 pcs. ⅜ × 4¾ × 5½, top and bottom
2 pcs. ⅜ × 4¼ × 5½, sides
2 pcs. ⅜ × 4¼ × 4, ends

Chase or scrape the line pattern using the process shown in Figure 8. Then make feet ⅝ in. long of ¼-in. dowel, shaped to the pattern shown. Set them into holes drilled into the bottom.

Fig. 25. Box No. 3.

Box No. 4 — Figure 26

Box, Figure 26, is 2½ by 4¼ by 5 in. over-all. The sizes of parts to be made are:

2 pcs. ⅜ × 4¼ × 5, top and bottom
2 pcs. ⅜ × 1¾ × 5, sides
2 pcs. ⅜ × 1¾ × 3½, ends

Round corners to ¾-in. radius. The feet are made of ½-in. dowel, shaped as shown.

Fig. 26. Box No. 4.

Box No. 6 — Figure 10

Box, Figure 10, is 2 by $4\frac{1}{2}$ by 7 in. over-all. Cut the cover design out of a $\frac{3}{8}$ by $3\frac{1}{2}$ by 6-in. board with the jig or coping saw. Glue it to a work board, and model it with a file as shown in Figure 9. Then glue or nail the piece to the cover and sand it. The sizes of the parts to be made are:

2 pcs. $\frac{3}{8} \times 4\frac{1}{2} \times 7$, top and bottom
2 pcs. $\frac{3}{8} \times 1\frac{1}{4} \times 7$, sides
2 pcs. $\frac{3}{8} \times 1\frac{1}{4} \times 3\frac{3}{4}$, ends

Box No. 5 — Figure 27

Box, Figure 27, is 2 by $4\frac{1}{2}$ by 7 in. outside measurement. It is beveled by planing sides to $7\frac{1}{2}$ deg. after having set the nails safely below planing surface. The cover is fitted into a previously rabbeted top edge, the rabbet being $\frac{1}{4}$ in. wide by $\frac{1}{4}$ in. deep. The openings left by rabbeting are closed with wood after nailing. The sizes of parts to be made are:

1 pc. $\frac{1}{4} \times 4 \times 6\frac{1}{2}$, top
1 pc. $\frac{1}{2} \times 4\frac{1}{2} \times 7$, bottom
2 pcs. $\frac{1}{2} \times 1\frac{1}{2} \times 7$, sides
2 pcs. $\frac{1}{2} \times 1\frac{1}{2} \times 3\frac{1}{2}$, ends
File the feet as shown in Figure 13.

Fig. 28. Box No. 7.

Box No. 7 — Figure 28

Box, Figure 28, is 2 by 3 by 5 in. Cover is slotted and nailed shut, and feet are cut as shown in Figure 13. The sizes of parts to be made are:

2 pcs. $\frac{3}{8} \times 3 \times 5$, top and bottom
2 pcs. $\frac{3}{8} \times 1\frac{1}{4} \times 5$, sides
2 pcs. $\frac{3}{8} \times 1\frac{1}{4} \times 2\frac{1}{4}$, ends
Round off the top edges.

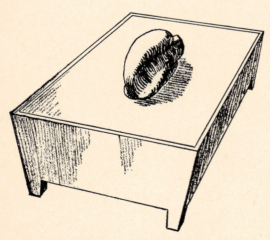

Fig. 27. Box No. 5.

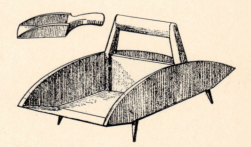

Fig. 29. Popcorn server and scoop.

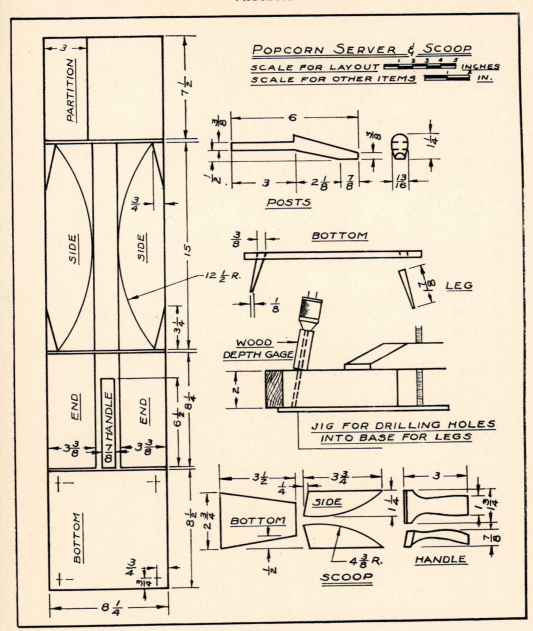

Plate 1.

Popcorn Server

(SEE PLATE 1 AND FIGURE 29)

This server also may be used as a fruit or sewing basket.

Material: Basswood

Stock size: $\frac{3}{8} \times 8\frac{1}{2} \times 40$, laid out as pictured.

Finish: Natural, in oil and wax

PROCEDURE

1. Use the plan of procedure described in Chapter 2. Make the following pieces as shown in Plate 1.
   1 bottom, $\frac{3}{8} \times 8\frac{1}{4} \times 8\frac{1}{2}$
   2 ends, $\frac{3}{8} \times 3\frac{3}{8} \times 8\frac{1}{4}$
   2 sides, $\frac{3}{8} \times 3\frac{3}{8} \times 15$, cut to pattern
   1 partition, $\frac{3}{8} \times 3 \times 7\frac{1}{2}$

1 handle, $\frac{3}{8} \times \frac{7}{8} \times 6\frac{1}{2}$, rounded as shown

2 posts, $1\frac{3}{16} \times 1\frac{1}{4} \times 6$, cut to pattern, and rounded

1 bottom of scoop, $\frac{3}{8} \times 2\frac{3}{4} \times 3\frac{1}{2}$, cut to pattern

2 sides of scoop, $\frac{3}{8} \times 1\frac{1}{4} \times 3\frac{3}{4}$

1 handle of scoop, $\frac{7}{8} \times 1\frac{3}{4} \times 3$

2. Drill holes into the bottom for feet, using jig and depth gauge as pictured. Drill through, inclining the drill toward each outer corner.

3. Round top edges of each endpiece and of the partition piece.

4. Surface plane and sand all pieces.

5. Using a $\frac{3}{8}$-in. dowel rod, mark off and taper four legs on the sanding disk, shaping them each from the full $\frac{3}{8}$ in. at the top to $\frac{1}{8}$ in. on the foot end. Cut them off after shaping to $1\frac{7}{8}$ in. long.

6. Nail sides to bottom, using No. 16 by 1-in. brads. Bevel the endpieces to join the bottom, and nail.

7. Assemble posts to the partition independently, fastening the handle last, then insert the unit, and nail to the server. Glue the legs into the holes.

8. Cut the scoop parts, thin and round

outer edges. Cut the handles, sand, nail, and finish.

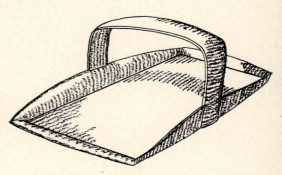

Fig. 30. Biscuit tray.

Hot-Biscuit Tray

(SEE PLATE 2 AND FIGURE 30)

Material: Basswood

Stock sizes: $\frac{3}{8} \times 6\frac{1}{2} \times 12\frac{1}{2}$; $\frac{1}{2} \times 3\frac{1}{4} \times 7\frac{1}{2}$; $\frac{3}{4} \times 4\frac{1}{2} \times 13\frac{1}{2}$

Finish: Natural, in oil and wax

PROCEDURE

1. Plane the first piece to size $\frac{3}{8}$ by 6 by 12, using the procedure outlined in Chapter 2. Surface plane and sand this piece for the bottom.

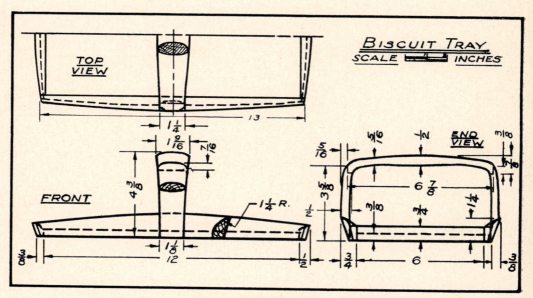

Plate 2.

2. Using the same procedure, make the posts and endpieces shown in Plate 2:
2 handle uprights $\frac{1}{2} \times 1\frac{1}{4} \times 3\frac{5}{8}$, tapered on both sides to $1\frac{1}{8}$ in. width at bottom end and fitted into side notches.
2 end pieces $\frac{1}{2} \times \frac{3}{4} \times 6$, rounded on inner edge.

3. Make the sides and handle in the same way:
2 tray sides $\frac{3}{4} \times 1\frac{1}{4} \times 13$, rounded on inner top edges except in the areas of end joints, and where the sides are notched to receive handle posts.
1 handle, $\frac{7}{8} \times 1\frac{9}{16} \times 6\frac{7}{8}$, cut to the contour shown in Plate 2.

4. Assemble sides and ends to bottom, cut lap joints into tops of the posts for the handle and assemble handle to tray with glue and nails.

5. When glue is dry, finish rounding inside corners of tray so that the side moldings meet the rounding of the end moldings at 45 deg.

6. Bevel outside faces of ends and sides.

7. File posts and handle to oval section.

8. Sand all over and finish as in Chapter 4.

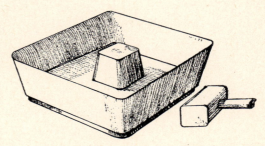

Fig. 31. Nut bowl and mallet.

Nut Bowl and Mallet
(SEE PLATE 3 AND FIGURE 31)

Material: Basswood or white pine
Stock size: $\frac{1}{2} \times 7\frac{1}{2} \times 22$, plus a $1\frac{5}{8} \times 2 \times 4\frac{5}{8}$ block for anvil and mallet
Finish: Natural, in oil and wax

PROCEDURE

1. Following the procedure described in Chapter 2, make the following pieces shown in Plate 3.
1 bottom, $\frac{1}{2} \times 7\frac{1}{4} \times 7\frac{1}{4}$

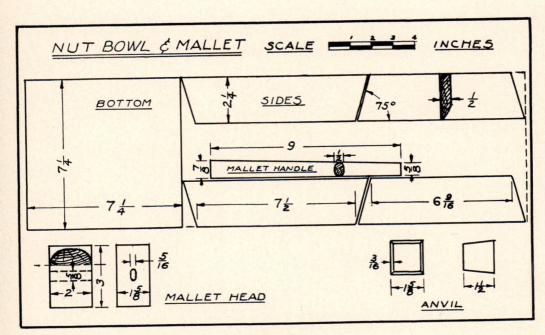

Plate 3.

4 sides, $\frac{1}{2} \times 2\frac{1}{4}$ as per pattern shown
1 anvil, $1\frac{5}{8} \times 1\frac{5}{8} \times 1\frac{1}{2}$, tapered and rounded as shown
1 mallet head, $1\frac{5}{8} \times 2 \times 3$, rounded and bored as shown
1 mallet handle, $\frac{1}{2} \times \frac{7}{8} \times 9$, tapered and rounded.

2. The ends of all sidepieces are cut at a 15-deg. angle, using the miter box or power saw. The dimensions given are for lengths on the short sides.

3. The two shorter pieces are pre-rounded on their inside top edges, while the long pieces are partially rounded, leaving the areas near the end joints for later finishing.

4. Surface plane and sandpaper; then assemble the long sides to the short, using No. 16 by $1\frac{1}{4}$-in. brads, three to a joint.

5. True the bottom as described in Chapter 3.

6. Nail on the bottom, two nails to the side.

7. Work down and finish inside corners of the top edge until the rounding of sides and ends meet at 45 deg.

8. Round outside corners as shown, and resand the box.

9. Fasten the anvil with screw from below. Also make the mallet, chiseling the eye from two $\frac{5}{16}$-in. holes. Fit the handle.

10. Finish all pieces with oil and wax.

Standing Photo Frame
(SEE PLATE 4 AND FIGURE 32)
6 × 8 inside dimensions

Material: Basswood
Stock size: $\frac{3}{8} \times 3 \times 19$
Finish: Natural, with rubbed oil and wax

PROCEDURE

1. Plane outside edges of piece of stock and rabbet both edges. Hold the plane at 60 deg. by means of a wood guide screwed or clamped to the plane as shown in Plate 4.

2. Lay out lines showing the width of all four pieces, and rip and plane to size.

3. Round the inside face of each piece, cutting a $\frac{1}{4}$ by $\frac{5}{8}$-in. chamfer, then

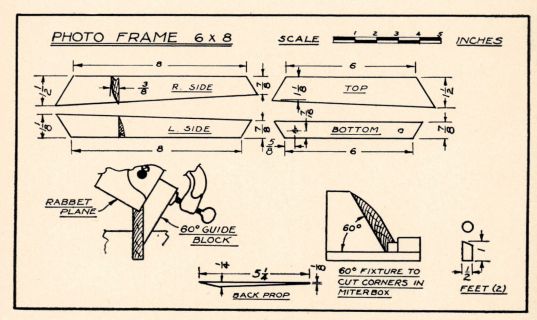

Plate 4.

Fig. 32. Photograph frame.

6. Make two legs out of $\frac{3}{8}$-in. dowel and cut the top angles as shown. Set a $\frac{3}{4}$-in. brad into the top of each and clip the heads. Then press the legs into the bottom member of the frame with glue.

7. Cut a Masonite backboard to size and add a hinged prop to the back of it, the prop made of a $\frac{1}{4}$-in. dowel sanded to a $\frac{1}{8}$-in. point below. The hinge is a piece of leather.

8. Finish as in Chapter 4.

Fig. 33. Shadow box.

Shadow Box
(SEE PLATE 5 AND FIGURE 33)
11×14-in. inside measurements
Material: Basswood

rounding both the resulting arrises, and sand both front and back.

4. Make a miter cutting jig of a 60-deg. block fixed to a base, which in turn is provided with a stop strip as shown in the sketch accompanying the detail for Plate 4. One end of each piece may now be set into the jig and cut, using a miter or power saw. Measure lengths on the short sides and cut all the opposite ends in the same manner.

5. To assemble, glue all joints and hold them with six or eight rounds of string. Push the string down over the frame to tighten. Weight the frame until set and reinforce with No. 18 by $\frac{3}{4}$-in. brads, one in each direction at each corner.

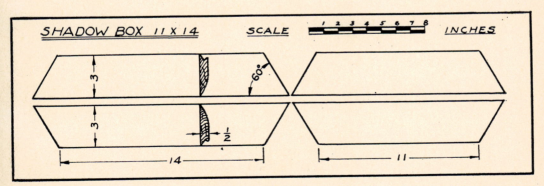

Plate 5.

Stock size: ⅜ × 7 × 34
Finish: Natural, clear lacquer and wax

PROCEDURE

1. Using the procedure outlined for the photo frame, Figure 32, gauge a 3-in. line from each rabbeted edge, rip and plane to size.
2. Plane a ³⁄₁₆ by 1-in. chamfer on front faces and plane the resulting arrises until their faces are slightly crowned, as shown in Plate 5. Sand all over.
3. Set into 60-deg. miter cutting jig and saw to dimensions given.
4. Assemble and finish as was done for the photo frame.

Twin Shadow Boxes
(SEE PLATE 6 AND FIGURE 34)

Material: Basswood

Stock size: ⅜ × 7 × 53
Finish: Natural as the foregoing.

PROCEDURE

1. Using the order of procedure in Chapter 2, make the following pieces:

Fig. 34. Twin shadow boxes.

2 pcs. ⅜ × 3 × 14, outer vertical sides
4 pcs. ⅜ × 3 × 12, tops and bottoms
4 pcs. ⅜ × 3 × 6¹³⁄₁₆, inside vertical sides

2. Surface plane all pieces, and nail parts together, using three No. 16 by 1-in. brads to a joint. Place nails into both ends of the 14-in. pieces, nailing them to the ends of the four 12-in. pieces. Then nail the 6¹³⁄₁₆-in. pieces to the other end of each 12-in. piece.

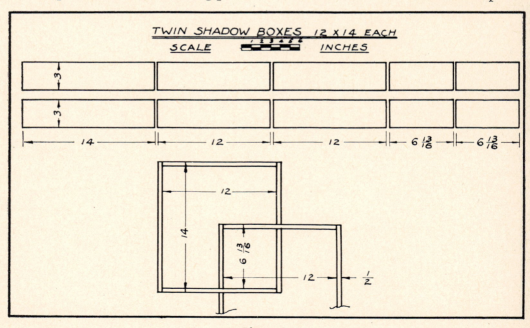

Plate 6.

You will now have two frames, each with a cut on one long side. Slip these together as shown, and nail through the middle of the 12-in. pieces into one end of the $6^{13}/_{16}$-in. pieces, holding the frame below it firmly down on the table corner and bending the upper short piece slightly inward while nailing.

3. Last, with a clamp over the remaining joint, keeping the pieces aligned, toe-nail from the inside corner into the loose short side, completing the frames. Finish all over.

Plant Box

(SEE PLATE 7 AND FIGURE 35)

Material: Basswood or mahogany
Stock sizes: $\frac{1}{2} \times 7 \times 17$ and $\frac{3}{8} \times 5 \times 12$
Finish: Natural, in rubbed oil

PROCEDURE

1. Plane both edges of $\frac{1}{2}$-in. stock and make the following pieces:

   2 sides, $\frac{1}{2} \times 3\frac{1}{8} \times 12$
   2 ends, $\frac{1}{2} \times 3\frac{1}{8} \times 4$

2. Of the $\frac{3}{8}$-in. stock make a bottom

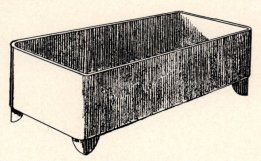

Fig. 35. Plant box.

$\frac{3}{8}$ by $4\frac{1}{2} \times 11\frac{1}{2}$, using the procedures outlined in Chapter 2.

3. Cut a $\frac{3}{8}$ by $\frac{1}{4}$ in. rabbet on side and end pieces. Plane a $\frac{3}{16}$ by $\frac{3}{4}$ in. chamfer on top inside face of ends only, and round as shown. Round sidepieces also except in the vicinity of the joints, which should be touched up after assembly. Surface plane and sand.

4. Nail sides to ends, using three No. 16 by $1\frac{1}{4}$-in. brads to the joint. Set nails deeply. Nail on the bottom.

5. Finish the inside corners, and sand them smooth, as shown in Plate 7.

6. Mark off the outside corner curves and plane them as in Figure 35, start-

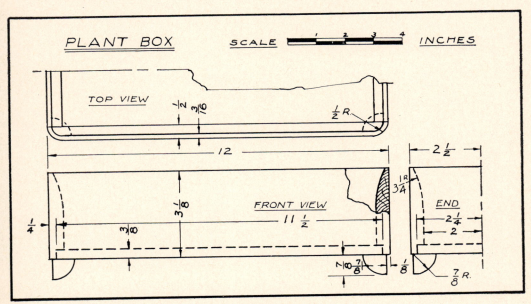

Plate 7.

ing with a measured chamfer. Then sand.

7. Feet are shaped on the end of a stick, rounded as shown and cut off. They are fastened with nails driven partly into them, clipped, and pressed with glue into the bottom. Finish as per directions in Chapter 4.

Desk Boxes

(SEE PLATE 8 AND FIGURES 36, 37, AND 38)
Material: Cherry, tulipwood, or basswood
Stock sizes: Lengths 1¼ in. long glued into a block 4 by 6 in., grain running vertically; bottom piece, ³⁄₁₆ × 4 × 6; top, ¼ × 3½ × 5½
Finish: Natural, in oil and wax

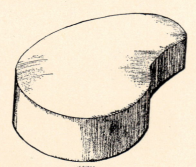

Fig. 36. Desk box.

PROCEDURE

1. True up the top and bottom faces of the block and mark the outside design

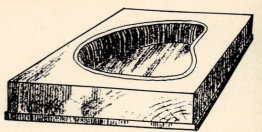

Fig. 37. Method of cutting out the walls of the desk boxes.

of box in the center of the top face. Then lay out the inside shape, making the thickness of the wall ³⁄₁₆ in.

2. Cut along the inside line with a coping or jig saw, and file and sand the inside surface to a high finish. See Figure 37.

3. Sand upper surface of bottom piece and glue to body, guarding against glue entering the inside area.

4. Cut outside of body and sand to a high finish.

5. Cut cover to fit, and rout the edge

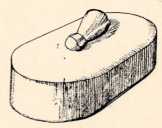

Fig. 38. Desk box.

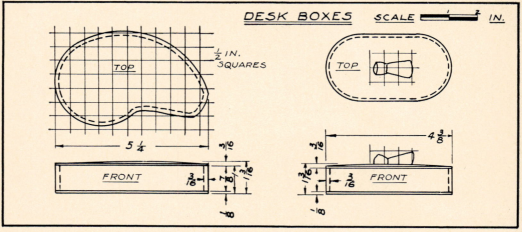

Plate 8.

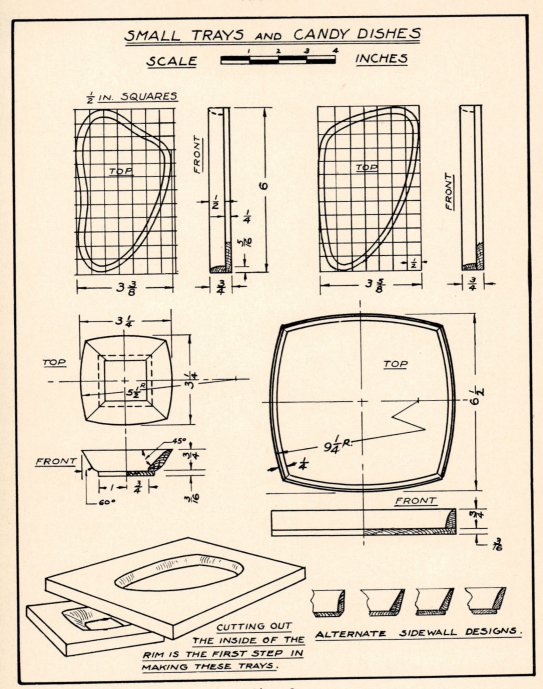

SMALL TRAYS AND CANDY DISHES

SCALE INCHES

½ IN. SQUARES

CUTTING OUT THE INSIDE OF THE RIM IS THE FIRST STEP IN MAKING THESE TRAYS.

ALTERNATE SIDEWALL DESIGNS.

Plate 9.

to slightly enter the box. Sand the top as shown. Make a knob from the inside waste, shaping it freely. Then finish the box all over.

The second desk box detailed in Plate 8 and illustrated in Figure 38 may be made by the same methods used for the one just described.

Small Trays and Candy Dishes

(SEE PLATE 9 AND FIGURES 39, 40, 41, AND 42)

Material: Mahogany, cherry, basswood, tulipwood, or fruit wood

Stock sizes: $\frac{1}{2} \times 4\frac{1}{2} \times 7$, for trays shown in Figures 39 and 40; $1 \times 4\frac{1}{2} \times 4\frac{1}{2}$, for tray in Figure 41; $1 \times 7\frac{1}{2} \times 7\frac{1}{2}$, for tray in Figure 42; $\frac{1}{4} \times$ above sizes for tray bottoms

Finish: Natural, in oil and wax

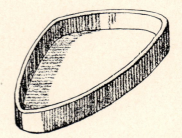

Fig. 40. Small irregular-shaped tray.

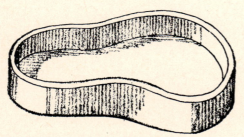

Fig. 39. Small irregular-shaped tray.

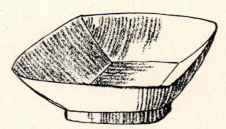

Fig. 41. Small irregular-shaped tray.

PROCEDURE

1. Lay out the inside pattern of the tray on the center of the wood. Drill hole inside the line, insert saw blade and cut out the inner part. Then file smooth to the line, and curve the edge to the desired side-wall pattern. Next finish the inner surface glass smooth. See Figure 37.

   In the trays shown in Figures 41 and 42, the rounded inside walls meet at sharp angles.

2. By means of pencil and finger, draw a uniform line around what is to be the outside edge of the tray parallel to the inside cut, allowing for proper thickness of side walls.

   Before cutting, surface plane and sand both sides of the bottom piece and glue it to the upper piece, applying glue to the under surface of the latter. Clamp all around and wash off surplus glue with water.

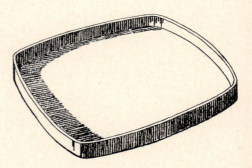

Fig. 42. Small irregular-shaped tray.

3. When the glue has set, remove clamps, and saw the outer shape down to the line. Then mark and bevel or round the outer wall as the pattern requires.

4. Finish as described in Chapter 4.

   This procedure lends itself to many variations.

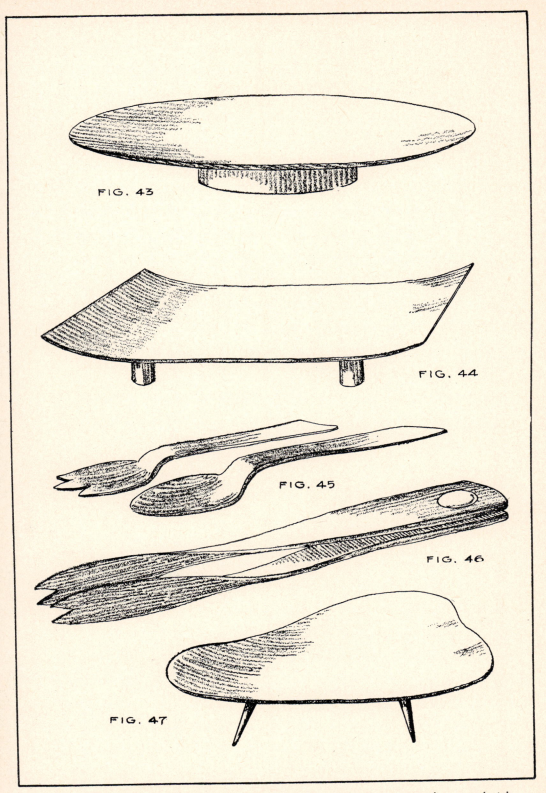

Fig. 43. Pressed circular sandwich plate; 44, pressed rectangular sandwich tray; 45, salad fork and spoon; 46, salad tongs; 47, free form pressed plate.

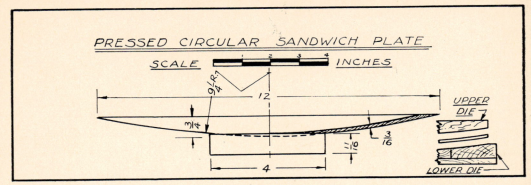

Plate 10.

Pressed Circular Sandwich Plate

(SEE PLATE 10 AND FIGURE 43)

Material: Basswood or birch, if solid wood, or any $\frac{1}{16}$-in. veneers, if built up

Stock sizes: 10-, 12-, or 14-in. disks in one piece

Finish: Natural, in oil and wax

PROCEDURE

1. Turn or hand cut upper and lower wood dies to shape shown in Plate 10, at least ¾ in. deep at center. Use 1½-in. hardwood stock for dies and oil them thoroughly after turning. If made by hand, cut the concave side as a ring and the other as a smooth convex piece.

2. Place the stock to be pressed into a closely covered dishpan, resting on a bent wire stand above the water, and steam it for thirty minutes. Then set the steamed piece between two sheets of household aluminum foil and into the dies. Clamp until dry. The drying may require several days.

   If the stock to be used is thin veneer, steam at least three sheets at once, remove from pan, coat inside faces with glue, set grains of each layer in opposition, and proceed as above. Use letter presses, drill presses, or wood clamps for pressing.

3. When dry, trim the outer edge and sand the pressed piece thoroughly.

4. Make a base, hollowed slightly to fit the bottom of the plate, and glue the two together.

5. Finish as in Chapter 4.

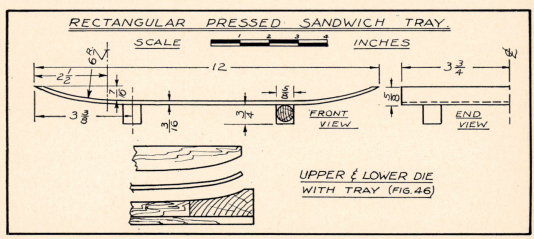

Plate 11.

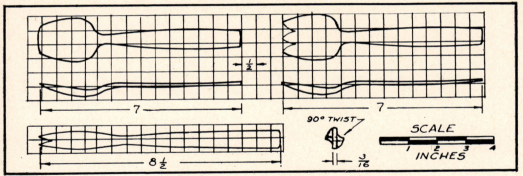

Plate 12. Details of salad fork, spoon, and tongs.

Rectangular Pressed Sandwich Tray

(SEE PLATE 11 AND FIGURE 44)

Material: Basswood, birch, mahogany, or cherry

Stock sizes: $\frac{3}{16} \times 7\frac{1}{2} \times 12$ and $\frac{5}{8}$ dowel, 3 in. long

Finish: Natural

PROCEDURE

1. The wood dies for the pressing of this tray are 7½ by 12 in., curving upward at each end. The curve begins at a point 2½ in. from the end and rises 7/16 in. on a 6-in. radius. The upper die is a single wood block. The lower die is built up of four pieces, shown in the sketch, Plate 10, the rounded parts of which can be sawed at 60 deg. across a 10-in. circular saw, ⅛ in. at a time.

2. Oil the dies and cut the tray stock, then steam, press between aluminum foil, clamp, and dry for several days.

3. Cut and attach the feet with glue. Then trim, oil, and finish.

Pressed Salad Fork, Spoon, and Tongs

(SEE PLATE 12 AND FIGURES 45 AND 46)

Material: Basswood, birch, or mahogany

Stock sizes: $\frac{3}{16} \times$ sizes given

Finish: Natural, in rubbed oil

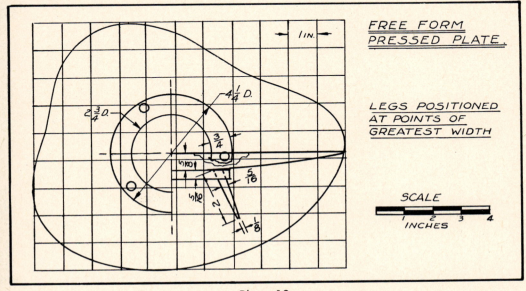

Plate 13.

PROCEDURE

1. Cut stock in approximate oversizes, steam, press into preshaped wood forms, clamp, and dry as previously described. The tongs are slightly cupped and each part is twisted 90 deg. at points favorable to practical closure of tines. Use a brass rivet for the hinge.
2. Finish in rubbed oil.

Free-Form Pressed Plate
(SEE PLATE 13 AND FIGURE 47)

Material: Basswood, birch, or mahogany
Stock sizes: $\frac{3}{16} \times 9 \times 11$; wood ring, $\frac{5}{16} \times 4\frac{1}{4}$; and dowel, $\frac{5}{16} \times 6$
Finish: Natural, in rubbed oil and wax

PROCEDURE

1. Cut form to pattern, steam, press, dry in clamps, and sand, using the directions and the dies of pressed plate in Figure 43.

2. Turn or cut a $4\frac{1}{4}$-in. diameter ring with $2\frac{3}{4}$-in. open center, in which the holes for feet have been previously bored. Use $\frac{5}{16}$-in. dowels for the feet, disk sanded to $\frac{1}{8}$-in. point and glued into the ring, which in turn is glued to the plate. Sand, oil, and wax.

Telephone-Directory Cover
(SEE PLATE 14 AND FIGURE 48)

Material: Basswood
Stock size: $\frac{3}{8} \times 10 \times 23$
Finish: Natural

PROCEDURE

1. Plane both edges of the board and square both ends. Making use of the procedure shown in Chapter 2, cut out the following pieces:
2 backstrips, $\frac{3}{8} \times \frac{5}{8} \times 11$, each drilled with four holes as shown
2 pcs. $\frac{3}{8} \times 8\frac{3}{16} \times 11$, top and bottom

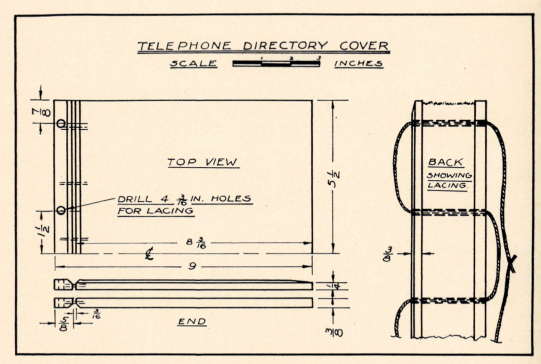

Plate 14.

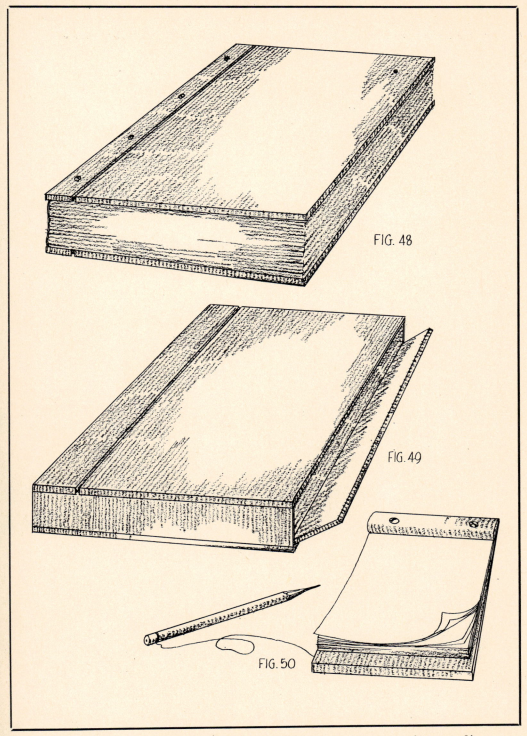

Fig. 48. Telephone-directory cover; 49, letter, recipe, or clipping file; 50, paper-pad board.

2. Surface plane all pieces.

3. Cut a ⅛ by ½-in. chamfer around three sides of top and bottom pieces and round toward a ¼-in. thickness on the three edges as shown.

4. Hinge edges are slightly chamfered as indicated. All are sanded.

5. Hinges are made of cotton cord anchored into drilled holes with glue and wood pegs. For lacing, drill holes through telephone book, holding the latter between wood strips while drilling. Lace with cord or tape, weaving end cords under lacing, and tie.

The same cover may be used for making a scrap or stamp book. Altering the dimensions shown, this cover also may be made into a guest or project book.

Letter, Recipe, or Clipping File
(SEE PLATE 15 AND FIGURE 49)

Material: Basswood

Stock sizes: ⅜ × 9 × 24½ and ³⁄₁₆ Masonite 9½ × 12¼

Finish: Natural

PROCEDURE

1. Plane two edges and one end, and cut out the following pieces according to directions in Chapter 2.
   1 cover, ⅜ × 8⅝ × 12¼
   1 backstrip, ⅜ × ¾ × 12¼
   2 sides, ⅜ × 1¹⁵⁄₁₆ × 11½
   2 ends, ⅜ × 1¹⁵⁄₁₆ × 9½
   1 pc. Masonite as given

2. Surface plane and sand all pieces.

3. Nail ends to back, using three No. 16 by 1-in. brads to a joint. Nail bottom to the above, using three No. 18 by ¾-in. brads to a side. Nail ¾-in. strip to rear top.

4. Glue a ¾-in. tape or strip of muslin against the hinge edges of cover and front. Then fold the flap, insert a strip of paper, apply glue, and press the second half of cloth against the box, keeping glue away from the fold of the hinge. Plane off surplus wood on flap until it closes.

5. A snap may be made of thin brass, screwed to inside of flap and bent outward to catch over a small screw-

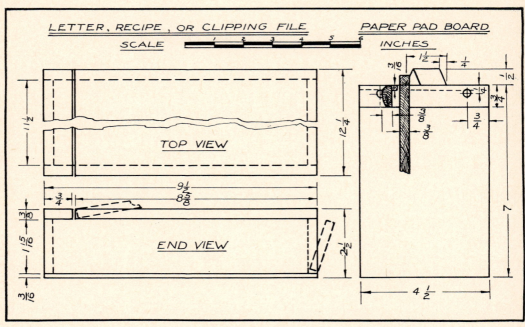

Plate 15.

head on the underside of the cover. An outside hook may also be used.

6. Finish all over as described in Chapter 4.

Paper-Pad Board
(SEE PLATE 15 AND FIGURE 50)

Material: Basswood

Stock size: $\frac{3}{8} \times 6 \times 7\frac{1}{2}$

Finish: Natural

PROCEDURE

1. Plane both edges and one end of stock and make:
   1 pc., $\frac{3}{8} \times 4\frac{1}{2} \times 7\frac{1}{2}$, marking out the upper pattern. Cut, and file to line. Surface plane and sand. See Plate 15.
   1 clamp piece, $\frac{3}{8} \times \frac{3}{4} \times 4\frac{1}{2}$, rounded on top and sanded.
2. Drill $\frac{3}{16}$-in. screw holes into clamp piece and $\frac{3}{32}$-in. holes into lower piece at corresponding points half through from above, as shown. Fix a small $\frac{3}{16}$ by $\frac{3}{16}$-in. strip on the back of the clamp piece, inside, so that when paper is punched and screwed down under the clamp, pressure is exerted on the latter's front edge.
3. Finish all over.

Make-Up Box
(SEE PLATE 16 AND FIGURE 51)

Material: Basswood and birch veneer

Stock sizes: $\frac{3}{8} \times 7\frac{3}{4} \times 20$; veneer $\frac{3}{16} \times 8\frac{1}{2} \times 29$

Finish: Natural, in oil and wax, or paint in modern color, such as tropical green. The finish should be rubbed in any case. A fine lined monogram in a light shade of the base color would be suitable.

PROCEDURE

1. Plane two edges of stock and make the following pieces, using method described in Chapter 2:
   2 sides, $\frac{3}{8} \times 1\frac{7}{8} \times 12$
   2 ends, $\frac{3}{8} \times 1\frac{7}{8} \times 7\frac{1}{4}$

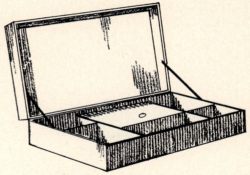

Fig. 51. Make-up box.

   2 partitions, $\frac{3}{16} \times 1\frac{1}{4} \times 4\frac{3}{8}$
   1 partition, $\frac{3}{16} \times 1\frac{1}{4} \times 11\frac{1}{4}$
   1 partition, $\frac{3}{16} \times 1\frac{1}{4} \times 2\frac{11}{16}$
   2 top and bottom veneer pieces, $\frac{3}{16} \times 8 \times 12$
   1 compartment cover in veneer, $\frac{3}{16} \times 4\frac{3}{8} \times 5\frac{1}{4}$
   1 cover, $\frac{3}{16} \times 2\frac{11}{16} \times 3\frac{1}{8}$
   16 triangular corner pieces, $\frac{1}{4} \times \frac{1}{4} \times 1\frac{1}{8}$
   2 pcs., $\frac{1}{4} \times \frac{3}{8} \times 7\frac{1}{4}$, bead mirror molding
   2 pcs., $\frac{1}{4} \times \frac{3}{8} \times 11\frac{1}{4}$, molding
2. Surface plane and sand first four pieces. Surface plane one side of partition pieces, gauge line $\frac{3}{16}$ in. all around edges, and plane to thickness, and sand.
3. Bore finger holes into cover pieces and sand smooth all over.
4. Nail long sides to short, using three No. 16 by 1-in. brads to the joint, avoiding the space reserved for resawing. See Figure 23.
5. Nail bottom and top, using three No. 18 by $\frac{3}{4}$-in. brads to the side, but do not set the heads until after resawing.
6. Gauge two lines for resawing, as shown in Figure 23, one $\frac{3}{4}$ in. and the other $\frac{7}{8}$ in. from the top face. Rip between lines, then plane to lines, as described in Chapter 3. See Figure 18.
7. Sand the entire box.
8. Triangular corner strips are cut on

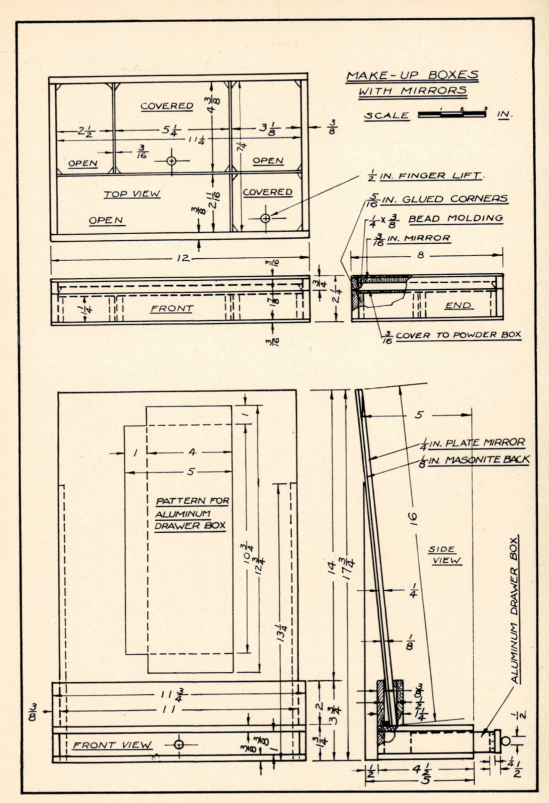

Plate 16.

the power saw, or, if the latter is not available, they may be ripped from the corners of stock presquared so that nothing remains but the smoothing of faces. Cut lengths and smooth top ends. Then apply glue and rub the corner strips into joints while partitions are held in their respective places. Wash out surplus glue.

9. Brass butt hinges are set into the box and cover. A 5-in. chain holds the cover open at the proper angle.

10. The mirror is ordered cut to close size and set into the cover. It is to be held in place with bead molding, mitered and nailed, the mirror resting on a soft cushion of cloth or paper.

11. Finish as suggested in Chapter 4.

Make-Up Mirror and Drawer

(SEE PLATE 16 AND FIGURE 52)

Material: Basswood or mahogany

Stock sizes: $\frac{3}{8} \times 9\frac{1}{2} \times 25$ and $\frac{1}{2} \times 1\frac{1}{2} \times 12$; Masonite $\frac{1}{8} \times 11 \times 16$; mirror of the same size; sheet aluminum 18 ga. $\times 5 \times 12\frac{3}{4}$ for the drawer

Finish: Natural

PROCEDURE

1. Plane both edges of the board, and following directions in Chapter 2, make the following pieces:
   2 pcs., $\frac{3}{8} \times 4\frac{1}{2} \times 11\frac{3}{4}$, top and bottom of drawer
   2 sides, $\frac{3}{8} \times 1 \times 4\frac{1}{2}$
   1 back, $\frac{3}{8} \times 1 \times 11$
   1 drawer front, $\frac{1}{2} \times 1 \times 11$
   2 mirror base pieces, $\frac{3}{8} \times 2 \times 11\frac{3}{4}$
   2 mirror base ends, $\frac{3}{8} \times \frac{1}{2} \times 2$
   2 mirror props, $\frac{3}{8} \times \frac{7}{8} \times 13\frac{1}{4}$, cut to the pattern shown
   1 drawer housing, No. $18 \times 5 \times 12\frac{3}{4}$ aluminum.

2. Surface plane and sand all pieces. Masonite is sanded on all edges and cemented to mirror with "Miracle

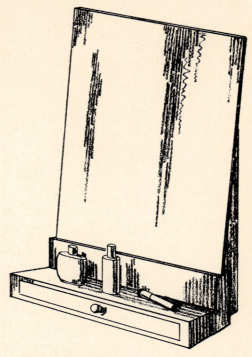

Fig. 52. Make-up box with mirror.

Cement," a rubber-base adhesive sold widely at hardware stores.

3. Assemble the mirror housing first, fastening the long pieces to the mirror housing ends with three No. 18 by $\frac{7}{8}$-in. brads and glue. Cement into the inside bottom of the housing a round rubber buffer, such as a single strand of standard electric cord. If this is oversize, file the Masonite until the space is just well filled.

4. Nail the sides to the back of the drawer boxing, then nail the top to these.

5. Next, nail the top of the drawer boxing to the bottom of the mirror housing, slanting the nails through the inside of the top piece.

6. Then nail the assembled unit to both mirror props, driving the topmost nail through the inside of the mirror housing at the top.

7. Nail the bottom to the box.

8. Cut a $\frac{1}{16} \times \frac{1}{4}$-in. rabbet around

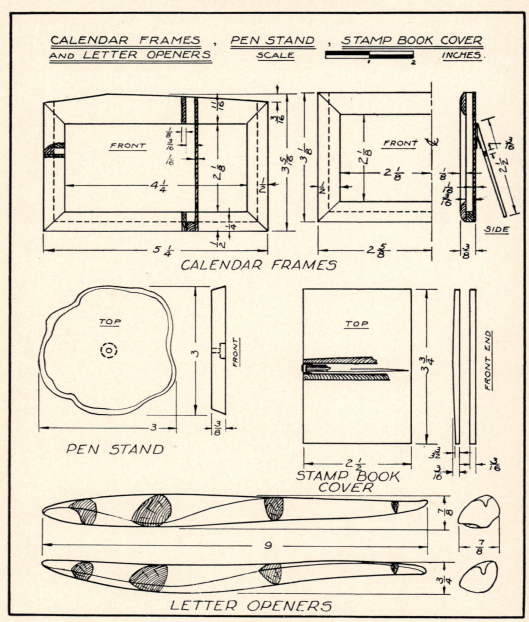

CALENDAR FRAMES , PEN STAND , STAMP BOOK COVER AND LETTER OPENERS — SCALE — INCHES.

CALENDAR FRAMES

PEN STAND

STAMP BOOK COVER

LETTER OPENERS

Plate 17.

three sides of the drawer front to allow for metal drawer sides and bottom. Use 18-ga. aluminum. Cut to the given size, smooth all edges with a file, and scribe a line $15/16$ in. parallel to each of the three edges. Cut out the squares thus marked at two corners, and bend on the scribed lines.

Clamp the metal between two hardwood blocks set to the lines, and with another block held full length along the metal, drive it down tight. If corners do not close, tap them together with a mallet.

9. Mark and punch nail holes and assemble drawer. Provide a knob. Fin-

ish all over as described in Chapter 4.

10. Set the mirror into the housing. Fill front opening with a wedge-shaped insert, which should be made to fit snugly. Finish it and then lightly force it into place with glue.

Calendar Frame
(SEE PLATE 17 AND FIGURE 53)

Material: Basswood, mahogany, cherry, or tulipwood

Stock sizes: ½ × 1 × 19 and $\frac{1}{16}$ × $3\frac{5}{16}$ × 5¼ veneer

Finish: Natural, in oil and wax

PROCEDURE

1. Cut veneer with a knife against a straightedge. If no other is available, berry box veneer will do.
2. Plane ½-in. stock on one edge, surface plane both faces, and gauge all around its edges ⅛ in. from one face and $\frac{3}{16}$ in. from the other. Rip between these lines and plane to lines against a bench stop.
3. Mark the given design on one end of the ⅛-in. thick piece and cut out. Mark and plane the remainder to ½-in. width. Out of the latter, cut two upright pieces 3⅛ in. long, and one bottom piece 5¼ in. long, mitering the lower corners at 45 deg., and the upper to agree with the angle of the top corners. Cut these angles by fixing the pieces, corners lapping, to a work board and saw the proper miters with a fine-toothed backsaw held against a guide block.
4. Gauge a ¼-in. line on the $\frac{3}{16}$-in. strip and saw and plane to the line. Cut the following pieces:
1 bottom strip, $\frac{3}{16}$ × ¼ × 4¾
2 side strips, $\frac{3}{16}$ × ¼ × 3⅛
5. Glue the side strips to the veneer as shown. Glue the top strips over these, putting glue into the mitered joints, and clamp to work board, distributing pressure uniformly. When set, round left and right sides as pictured, and

finish all over. Oil and wax. Make a back prop and hinge with leather.

The space left open back of the top crosspiece is for the insertion of calendar cards which may be purchased at a stationery store.

Second Calendar Frame
(SEE PLATE 17 AND FIGURE 54)

Material and Finish: Same as for frame shown in Figure 53

Stock sizes: ½ × ⅝ × 19 and $\frac{1}{16}$ × 3⅛ × 5¼ veneer

PROCEDURE

1. The stock is planed and cut as for frame in Figure 54, the piece ⅛ in. thick being planed to ½-in. width, and that $\frac{3}{16}$ in. thick to ¼-in. width. See Plate 17.
2. Make the following pieces:
2 top and bottom, ⅛ × ½ × 5¼, mitered to 45 deg. at each end
2 sides, ⅛ × ½ × 3⅛, mitered likewise
1 bottom spacer, $\frac{3}{16}$ × ¼ × 4¾, square ends
2 side spacers, $\frac{3}{16}$ × ¼ × 3⅛, square ends
3. Round the front pieces of the frame as shown in Plate 17.
4. Assemble, using procedure described for Figure 53. Provide a back prop made of a piece of ¼-in. dowel fixed to the back with a leather hinge.
5. Finish all over in oil and wax.

Pen Stand
(SEE PLATE 17 AND FIGURE 55)

Material: Cut a piece of hardwood of an interesting section and grain, from a bough of an apple or pearwood tree

Finish: Natural, in oil and wax

PROCEDURE

1. After selecting a suitable section of wood ⅜ in. thick, remove the bark without injuring the layer immediately under it. This furnishes an in-

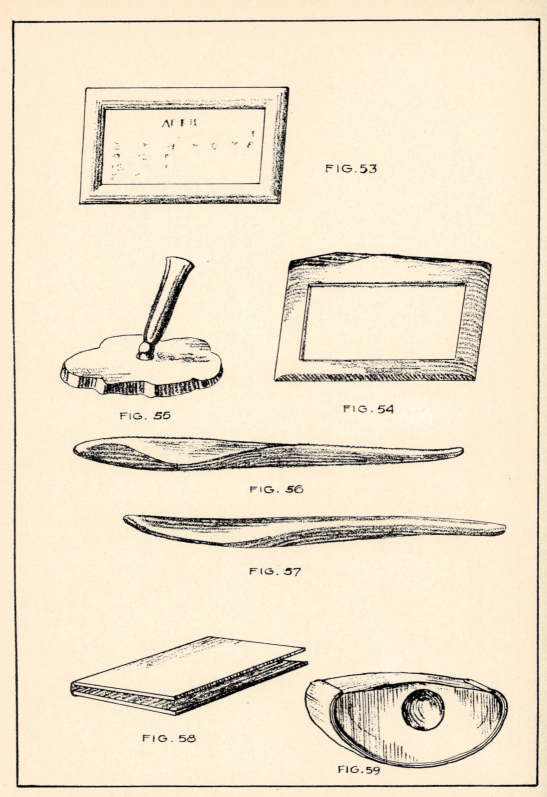

FIG. 53

FIG. 55

FIG. 54

FIG. 56

FIG. 57

FIG. 58

FIG. 59

Fig. 53. Calendar frame; 54, calendar frame No. 2; 55, pen stand; 56 and 57, unique letter openers; 58, stamp book; 59, roller blotter.

teresting, clean, outer rim. Finish the top and bottom face of the section on a sanding wheel if possible. Oil and wax.

2. Drill and counterbore the wood from below and attach a pen socket. See Plate 17. The latter may be obtained from a stationery store.

Letter Openers
(SEE PLATE 17 AND FIGURES 56 AND 57)

Material: Mahogany, rosewood, fruit wood, boxwood, or walnut

Stock size: ⅞ × ⅞ × 9

Finish: Natural, in oil and wax

PROCEDURE

1. The purpose is to produce a free form, rhythmic pattern, interesting to feel and to look at. Saw out any desired shape, ripping the stock down each side to give a blunt point. Do the same to a lesser degree on the handle end, and repeat the ripping on the adjacent sides. You then have the desired form in the square. See Plate 17.

2. Proceed with a rasp, following no pattern, intending merely to produce an interesting handle and blade. Try for simplicity, flow of line, invention of form, pleasant *feel*, and refinement. Start by rasping in an oblique direction, carrying the resulting groove into an imperceptible fade-out toward each side, as the illustrations suggest. The arrises thus formed by the rasp may be of use in the design.

The system of rhythmic and free invention may also be applied to flat surfaces, as on covers of boxes, or on the stamp-book cover, shown in Figure 58.

Stamp Book
(SEE PLATE 17 AND FIGURE 58)

Material: Any wood with interesting grain

Stock size: ½ × 3 × 4

Finish: Natural

PROCEDURE

1. Plane one edge and proceed to work the wood to size by the method described in Chapter 2. See Plate 17. Surface plane each face and gauge all around the piece 3/16 in. from each face. Rip between lines and plane the pieces to the thickness marked.

2. Sand all over, slightly crowning the top, as shown in Plate 17.

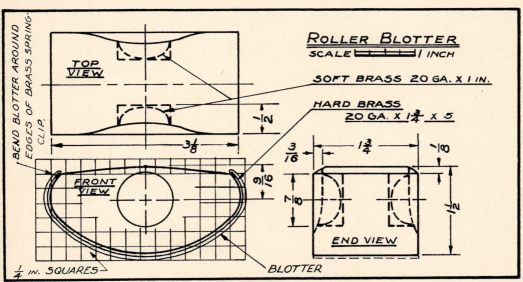

Plate 18.

3. Lay the pieces, inside faces up, ¼ in. apart and apply the back hinge by gluing a ¾-in. strip of cloth or leather over the joint, the glue being applied to the wood. Wash off all surplus glue.

4. Oil and wax the wood.

5. Fold four pieces of 4 by 9½-in. heavy paper into two equal parts and slip one inside the other, book fashion. Press them down and cut the pack to size 4⅜ by 3½ in. Fold 2 in. of each page forward on itself and crease tightly.

6. Stitch the folded pack into the back of the book with thread.

Roller Blotter
(SEE PLATE 18 AND FIGURE 59)

Material: Basswood, mahogany, cherry, or tulipwood, and sheet brass

Stock sizes: wood, 1½ × 1¾ × 3⅛; sheet brass — hard, 20-ga. × 1¾ × 5; 2 pcs., sheet brass — half hard, 20-ga. × 1 in. diameter

Finish: Natural, in oil and wax

PROCEDURE

1. Plane wood on both outside faces.

2. Mark center on both faces and bore a ⅞-in. hole, ½ in. deep on both centers, using depth gauge.

3. Mark the front view design on both faces. See design on Plate 18. Cut and work to layout lines.

4. Mark ³⁄₁₆-in. depth around the inside edge of each hole, and carve and finish both faces to the line, narrowing the block slightly at the area of handling. The carving extends to a ridge around the hole approximately ½ in. from the rocker edge. The ridge is then rounded down.

5. Finish and oil the wood. See Chapter 4.

6. Raise the brass disks to bowl shape with a ball-peen hammer over a depression on the end of a wooden hammering block. Press the finished brass

pieces into the ⅞-in. bored holes on each face, concave side out, cementing them with rubber-base linoleum-type cement. If the brass rests below the edge of the wood, round the latter.

7. Bend the sheet of hard brass carefully over a steel bar with a wood mallet, curving it to fit snugly around the blotter face of the block. The brass with blotter, size 1¾ by 8 in., bent around its ends, should snap over the wood and hold it without slipping.

Crumb Brush
(SEE PLATE 19 AND FIGURE 60)

Material: Mahogany, cherry, or fruit wood

Stock size: ⅝ × 2 × 9

Finish: Oil and wax

PROCEDURE

1. Plane a working edge on the length of the stock piece and mark off the piece through which the brush fibers are to be strung: ¼ in. from working edge, cut off and plane. Then reduce its width to ½ in., sand outside faces, and round its edges.

2. Make a handle of the remaining stock, planing the thickness of the lower sides to fit against the ½-in. width of the first piece. Then shape the remainder into a free form, as suggested in the illustration.

3. File and sand all over as explained in Chapter 4.

4. Returning to the first piece, mark out two rows of holes as shown in Plate 19. Center-punch each hole carefully, and drill ⁵⁄₃₂-in. holes to a depth of ³⁄₁₆ in., using a depth gauge. See Plate 1. Use a sharp drill ground to scrape, and feed carefully, not to split the surface. A drill press running at top speed is best. Next, drill the ³⁄₃₂-in. holes through the ⁵⁄₃₂-in. holes as shown.

5. Using a lining chisel, carve a groove on the upper face, running from one

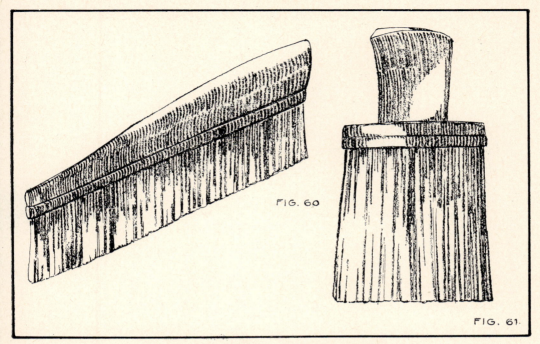

Fig. 60. Crumb brush; 61, hat brush.

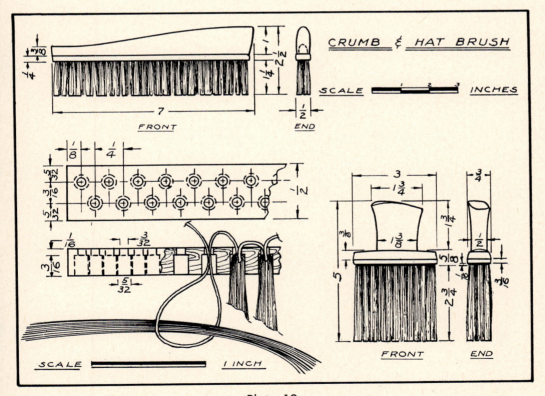

Plate 19.

$\frac{3}{32}$-in. hole to the other, just deep enough to hold the binding wire. This groove is not shown on Plate 19. Where the wire is shown arching above the wood, it should actually rest in the groove so that the handle piece may be glued to its flat surface.

6. Purchase either hair or fiber from a local brush manufacturer, or obtain it through a school supply house. The brush shown was made with a 3-in. length fiber.

7. Annealed No. 26 brass wire may be purchased from a metal supply source.

8. Make the brush, threading a 24-in. length of wire through the end hole from the top and back again. Draw the wire through into a loop as shown. Lay a sufficient quantity of hair into the loop and pull up the wire until the hair seats itself, just filling the hole. The upper wire is then directed into the groove as mentioned, and the entire operation is repeated on all the brush tufts all the way around. Secure the end wires by twisting the two together, and flatten all down.

9. Glue the handle to the brush and clamp until dry.

10. Cut the hair to uniform length by laying them over a razor blade set upright in a vise and hitting down on them with a softwood block or mallet.

11. Finish the wood all over, and oil and wax.

Hat Brush
(SEE PLATE 19 AND FIGURE 61)

Material and Finish: As for first brush
Stock sizes: $1 \times 1 \times 4$; $1 \times 1\frac{3}{4} \times 1\frac{3}{4}$ for handle

PROCEDURE

1. Plane both edges of stock, gauge $\frac{1}{4}$ in. from one side and $\frac{3}{8}$ in. from the other. Rip and plane to lines. Cut to length, square the ends, and round the corners slightly. Curve the top side of the $\frac{3}{8}$-in. piece as shown.

Drill a $\frac{3}{16}$-in. hole through the center of the top and countersink the underside.

2. Make a free-form handle with interesting lines, and glue and screw this to the $\frac{3}{8}$-in. piece.

3. Lay out and center-punch three rows of holes on the $\frac{1}{4}$-in. piece, staggered as shown in Plate 19. Then drill the holes and gouge out the grooves, ending on one of the outside rows.

4. Thread and draw the fiber as previously explained, and glue the upper and lower parts of the brush together. Sand the edge of the lower piece to a thickness of $\frac{3}{16}$ in., at the outer edge, tipping the sanding block to do so. Then cut the hair, and finish the wood of the brush as described in Chapter 4.

Reading Chair
(SEE PLATE 20 AND FIGURES 62 AND 63)

Material: Cherry, mahogany, or maple
Stock sizes: $1\frac{1}{8} \times 6 \times 78$; $1\frac{3}{4} \times 5 \times 35$; $1\frac{3}{4} \times 6 \times 45$ (crosspieces)
Finish: Natural, in oil and wax

PROCEDURE

1. Lay out side, leg, and back-post pieces, cut and plane to lines. Then using the procedure in Chapter 2, cut the crosspieces.

Parts to be made are as follows:
2 sides, $1\frac{1}{8} \times 6 \times 25\frac{5}{8}$, cut to pattern
2 back posts, $1\frac{1}{8} \times 3$ to $1 \times 25\frac{1}{2}$, cut to pattern
2 front legs, $1\frac{3}{4} \times 2\frac{1}{2}$ to $1 \times 16\frac{1}{2}$, cut to lap the side as shown. Use the formula given in the sketch in Plate 20.
2 back legs, $1\frac{3}{4} \times 3\frac{1}{4}$ to $1 \times 17\frac{1}{2}$, cut similar to the method used for the front legs
1 front crosspiece, $1\frac{3}{4} \times 3 \times 23\frac{1}{2}$, planed to curve downward to $1\frac{1}{8}$-in. thickness in the center, the underside curving upward to the sides and running parallel with the top

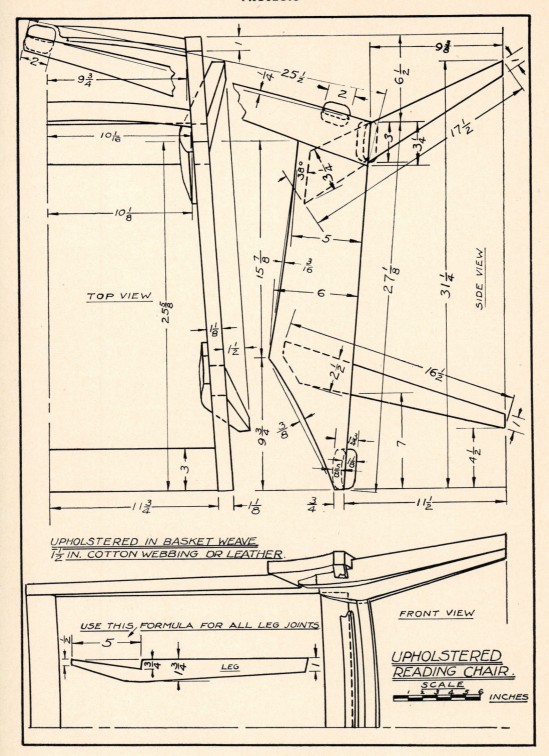

Plate 20.

Fig. 62. Upholstered reading chair.

1 back crosspiece, $1\frac{3}{4} \times 3 \times 20\frac{1}{4}$, cut to a shape similar to that used for the front crosspiece. See Plate 20.
1 back upper crossbar, $1\frac{3}{4} \times 2 \times 19\frac{1}{2}$, cut like the crosspieces
1 lower back crossbar, $1\frac{3}{4} \times 2 \times 20\frac{1}{8}$, also cut like the crosspieces

2. Mark the length on each crosspiece and back bar, set the saw at 4 deg., and cut both ends of the pieces, slanting each end inward to fit the sides of the chair as they decrease in width toward the back. Round all edges.

3. Fit sidepieces to back posts, bore both for dowels as explained in Chapter 3; then glue, dowel, and clamp them.

4. Taper the legs to 1-in. thickness at the floor, starting from a point just under the joint. Taper the part back of the lap to thin at the top, and round all edges. Drill and countersink five screw holes into the lap area, mark and drill corresponding pilot holes into the chair sides, and then glue and screw the legs into place. See Chapter 3.

5. Recut the back crosspiece to fit over the back leg; then bore dowel holes into the ends of all crosspieces, following the directions in Chapter 3, and bore corresponding holes into the sides and back posts. Glue, dowel, and clamp the chair. Wipe off surplus glue.

6. Round all sharp edges and finish the wood as in Chapter 4.

7. Tack webbing over the crosspieces, basket fashion. See Figures 62 and 63.

Fig. 63. Upholstered reading chair.

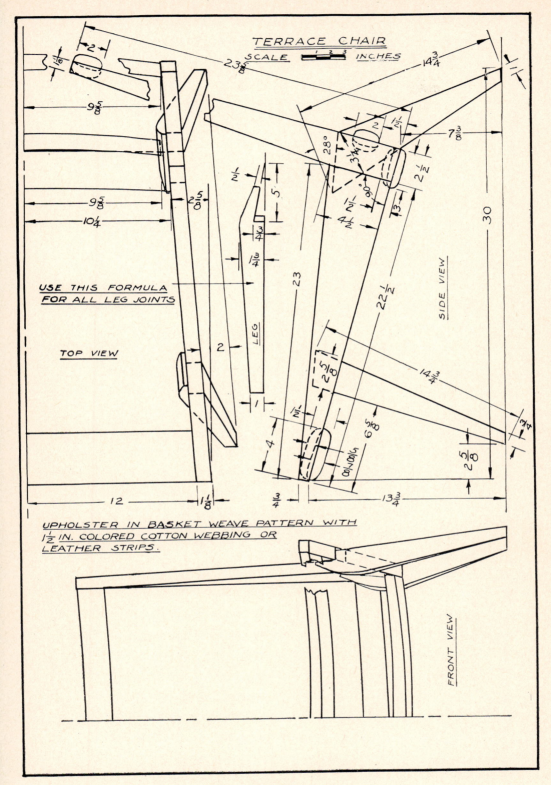

TERRACE CHAIR

Plate 21.

Fig. 64. Upholstered terrace chair.

Terrace Chair

(SEE PLATE 21 AND FIGURE 64)

Material: Cherry, mahogany, or maple
Stock sizes: $1\frac{1}{8} \times 6 \times 48$; $1\frac{3}{4} \times 5 \times 31$;
$1\frac{1}{2} \times 6 \times 45$
Finish: Natural, in oil and wax

PROCEDURE

1. Plane both edges of stock pieces and lay out the parts. Cut and plane to lines, making the following pieces:
   2 sides, $1\frac{1}{8} \times 4\frac{1}{2}$ to $\frac{3}{4} \times 22\frac{1}{2}$
   2 back posts, $1\frac{1}{8} \times 2\frac{1}{2}$ to $1\frac{1}{8} \times 23\frac{5}{8}$
   2 front legs, $1\frac{3}{4} \times 2\frac{5}{8}$ to $\frac{3}{4} \times 14\frac{3}{4}$
   2 back legs, $1\frac{3}{4} \times 3\frac{1}{2}$ to $1 \times 14\frac{3}{4}$
   1 front crosspiece, $1\frac{1}{2} \times 4 \times 24$, planed to curve downward to $\frac{7}{8}$ thickness in the center. The bottom of the piece curves upward toward the ends, parallel with the top
   1 back crosspiece, $1\frac{1}{2} \times 3 \times 20\frac{1}{2}$, planed as above
   1 upper back crossbar, $1\frac{1}{2} \times 2 \times 19\frac{1}{4}$, planed as above.

1 lower back crossbar, $1\frac{1}{2} \times 2 \times 19\frac{1}{2}$, planed as above

2. Mark the lengths of all crosspieces, set the power or miter-box saw to 4 deg., clamp the pieces to a straightedge, and cut both ends, slanting inward from the front.

3. Fit the chair sides to back posts, bore dowel holes, and glue, dowel, and clamp.

4. Taper all legs from a point under the joint to 1-in. thickness on the floor end.

5. Cut the upper leg lap joints $\frac{3}{4}$ in. deep and 5 in. face, as shown in the sketch in Plate 20.

6. Drill and countersink five screw holes into the lap area. Mark and drill corresponding pilot holes into the chair sides. Glue and screw legs to frame.

7. Recut back crosspiece to fit over back legs. Bore dowel holes into all crosspieces. Bore corresponding holes into chair sides and back posts. Glue, dowel, and clamp the chair.

8. Round all edges thoroughly and sand

Fig. 65. Shadow box.

the chair all over. Finish as directed in Chapter 4.

9. Tack 2- to 3-in. strips of leather, webbing, or folded plastic fabric in basket fashion over the frame, the cross webbing being tacked to an extra wood strip screwed to the lower edge of the sides. See Figure 64. Add cushions if desired.

Shadow Box

(SEE PLATE 22 AND FIGURE 65)

Material: Basswood or maple

Stock sizes: $\frac{1}{2} \times 6\frac{1}{2} \times 96$; $\frac{1}{2} \times 8 \times 39$

Finish: Natural, outside and front

PROCEDURE

1. Make the following pieces:
   1 top, $\frac{1}{2} \times 6 \times 39$, rabbeted $\frac{1}{4} \times \frac{1}{2}$ to hold backboard
   1 bottom, $\frac{1}{2} \times 6 \times 38$, rabbeted to fit backboard
   2 sides, $\frac{1}{2} \times 6 \times 8$, rabbeted to fit backboard
   1 back, $\frac{1}{2} \times 8 \times 38\frac{1}{2}$
2. Surface plane and sand all pieces.
3. Nail and glue top to sides, and sides to bottom. Then add back.
4. Finish the box, using a natural finish on the outside surfaces. Paint the inside. See Chapter 4.

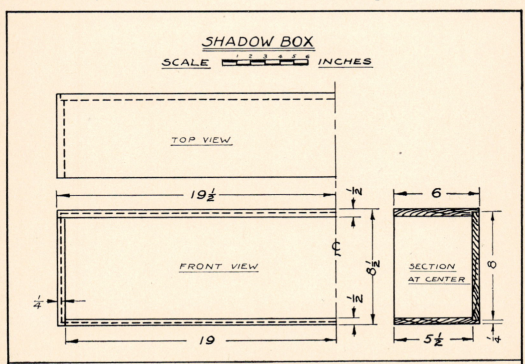

Plate 22.

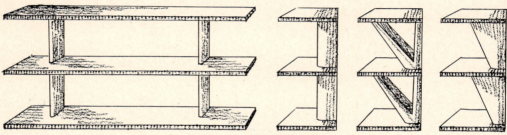

Fig. 66. Wall shelf.

A safe way to select color for furniture is to use one of the neutral tones to be found in drapery or upholstery material. At the date of writing, dark forest green and certain soft blue-greens are frequently used for this purpose.

Wall Shelves

(SEE PLATE 23 AND FIGURE 66)

Material: Basswood

Stock sizes: $\frac{1}{2} \times 6 \times 86$; $1 \times 2\frac{3}{4} \times 25$

Finish: Natural, in oil and wax

PROCEDURE

1. Make the following pieces:
   3 shelves, $\frac{1}{2} \times 5\frac{1}{2} \times 28\frac{1}{2}$
   4 vertical pieces, $1 \times 2\frac{1}{2} \times 6$, planed

to the section shown, and sanded. (Two alternate methods of separating the shelves are shown in Plate 19. Stock dimensions for these are not given here.)

2. Mark each shelf and plane a $\frac{1}{8} \times 1$-in. chamfer on undersides so that all front and side faces measure $\frac{3}{8}$ in. See Plate 23.

3. Surface plane and sand all pieces.

4. Drill and countersink screw holes into the shelves. Two screws put in from below hold each bracket on the bottom and center shelves; two screws put in downward from the top hold the top shelf; and one screw downward from the top at the front of

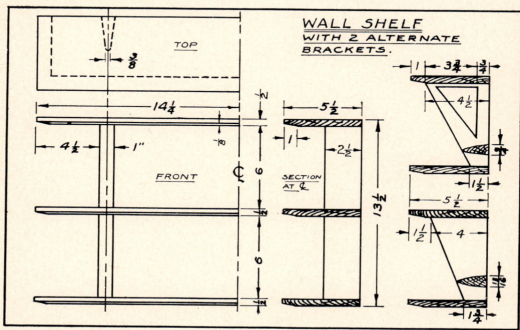

Plate 23.

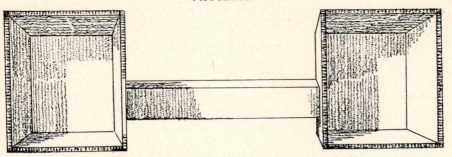

Fig. 67. Three-section shadow box and shelf.

the center shelf bracket, and a nail into the back of the same bracket complete the assembly. Assemble bottom and center shelves completely. Then add top.

5. Finish all over. See Chapter 4.

Three-Section Shadow Box
(SEE PLATE 24 AND FIGURE 67)

Material: Basswood, yellow poplar, or maple

Stock sizes: $\frac{1}{2} \times 5\frac{1}{2} \times 12$ ft; $\frac{1}{2} \times 4\frac{1}{2} \times 68$ in.

Finish: Outside and front face natural in oil and wax. The insides should be painted a neutral tone found in the drapery or upholstery used in the room. Dark forest green, or certain soft blue-greens also may be found satisfactory.

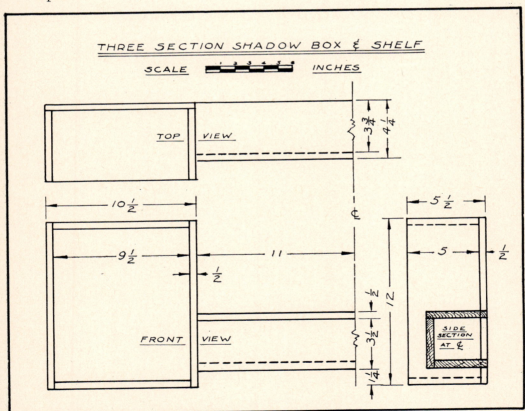

Plate 24.

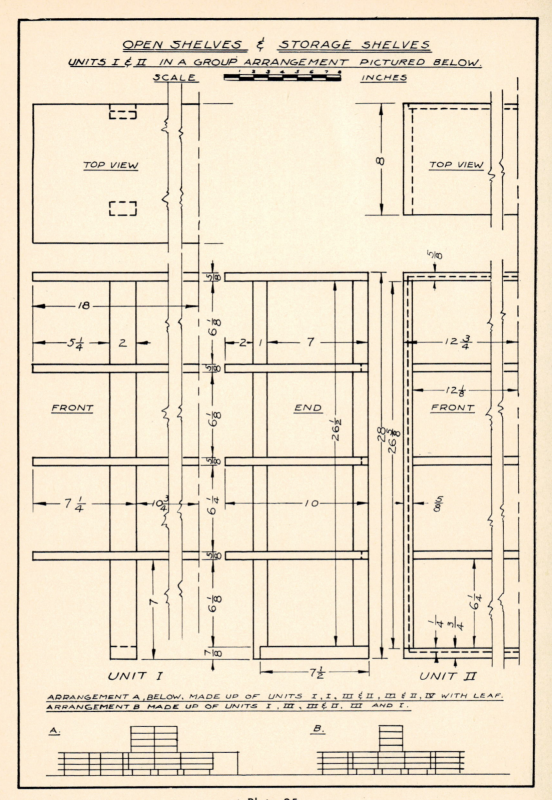

OPEN SHELVES & STORAGE SHELVES
UNITS I & II IN A GROUP ARRANGEMENT PICTURED BELOW.

ARRANGEMENT A, BELOW, MADE UP OF UNITS I, I, III & II, III & II, IV WITH LEAF.
ARRANGEMENT B MADE UP OF UNITS I, III, III & II, III AND I.

Plate 25.

PROCEDURE

1. Make the following pieces:
    4 sides, $\frac{1}{2} \times 5 \times 12$
    4 tops and bottoms, $\frac{1}{2} \times 5 \times 9\frac{1}{2}$
    2 backs, $\frac{1}{2} \times 10\frac{1}{2} \times 12$, made of two widths
    1 middle box top, $\frac{1}{2} \times 4\frac{1}{4} \times 22$
    1 front, $\frac{1}{2} \times 3\frac{1}{2} \times 22$
    1 bottom, $\frac{1}{2} \times 3\frac{3}{4} \times 22$
2. Surface plane and sand all pieces.
3. Glue and nail outer box sides to their tops and bottoms. Then fasten the backs with nails.
4. Glue and nail the middle box. Then nail it to the outer boxes through the inside walls of the latter. Fill all nail holes.
5. Sand and finish all over. See Chapter 4.

Open Shelves
(SEE PLATE 25 AND FIGURE 68)

(Unit I of a group in a built-up arrangement)

Material: Basswood, maple, or oak

Stock sizes: $\frac{5}{8} \times 10\frac{1}{4} \times 12\frac{1}{4}$ ft.; $1 \times 2 \times 11$ ft.

Finish: Outside natural, in oil and wax. Inside painted and rubbed, as described in the finishing of the shadow boxes

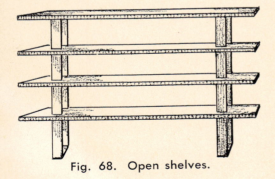

Fig. 68. Open shelves.

PROCEDURE

1. Make pieces below, using procedure in Chapter 2.
    4 shelves, $\frac{5}{8} \times 10 \times 36$
    4 post pieces, $1 \times 2 \times 6\frac{1}{8}$

2 post pieces, $1 \times 2 \times 6\frac{1}{4}$
2 posts, $1 \times 2 \times 7$, cut to lap floor pieces
2 posts, $1 \times 2 \times 26\frac{1}{2}$
2 floor pieces, $\frac{7}{8} \times 2 \times 7\frac{1}{2}$

2. Notch three lower shelves, 1×2, to fit rear posts. Drill posts for screws at shelf levels.
3. Drill the floor pieces for screws to go into the base posts. See Chapter 3. Drill each lower shelf for screws to go into the front posts above it. Then bore the upper shelf and those below it from beneath for dowels to be joined with the posts below it. Bore corresponding dowel holes into the posts.
4. Fasten the front base posts to the bottom shelf with glue and screws driven from the top down; then fasten the remaining base pieces, driving the screws through the rear post into the shelf from the back.
5. Fasten the second post to the second shelf by driving the screws from the top down; treat the third shelf in the same manner. Glue and dowel the top and each succeeding shelf to the front posts. Then fasten each shelf to the rear post in order, from the second to the top, gluing and clamping the top post last.
6. Turn the assembly top side down, and nail all doweled joints, driving the nails up from beneath.
7. Finish all over. See Chapter 4.

Storage Shelves
(SEE PLATE 25 AND FIGURE 69)

(Unit II of a group in a built-up arrangement, illustrated on Plate 25)

Material: Basswood, maple, or oak

Stock sizes: $\frac{5}{8} \times 8\frac{1}{4} \times 13$ ft.; $\frac{7}{8} \times 8\frac{1}{4} \times 26$ in.; $\frac{3}{8} \times 8\frac{1}{2} \times 7$ ft.

Finish: Outside and front faces natural, in oil and wax. Inside painted and rubbed, as described in the finishing of the shadow boxes

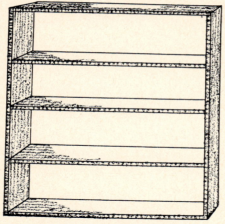

Fig. 69. Storage shelves.

PROCEDURE

1. Make the following pieces according to the directions given in Chapter 2:
   1 top, $\frac{5}{8} \times 8 \times 25\frac{1}{2}$, rabbeted to hold back panel
   1 bottom, $\frac{3}{4} \times 8 \times 25\frac{1}{2}$, rabbeted for back panel
   3 shelves, $\frac{5}{8} \times 7\frac{5}{8} \times 24\frac{1}{4}$
   2 sides, $\frac{5}{8} \times 8 \times 26\frac{5}{8}$, rabbeted for back panel
   1 back, $\frac{3}{8} \times 24\frac{3}{4} \times 27\frac{1}{8}$
2. Surface plane and sand all pieces.
3. Drill screw holes into the bottom piece where it is joined to the sides. Bore dowel holes into the shelves and at corresponding points at shelf levels into the sides. Also bore dowel holes into the upper end of sides with corresponding holes into the underside of the top.
4. Glue, dowel, and clamp all joints, and remove excess glue. Fasten on the bottom with screws, and nail the back into the case with brads.
5. Finish all over. See Chapter 4.

When the case just described is used as part of a composite arrangement, it may be applied in any of four ways:

1. Unit II may be the top member of a two-high combination with Unit III as the base member. See sketch at bottom of Plate 25.

2. It may be a floor unit in an arrangement where it stands with no base, the bottom shelf resting on the floor. The case is then standard height.

3. Unit II may also be a floor unit with a 7-in. base, using two $2 \times 7 \times 7$-in. blocks. At this level, the top is above the normal height line, adding interest to the group.

4. It may be a two-high unit, made up of two like cases, set one over the other. Their depth being 8 in., as compared with the greater depths of neighboring units, adds front-line interest to the arrangement.

Playroom Storage Case
(SEE PLATE 26 AND FIGURES 70 AND 71)

This case is shown in both 27-in., and 30-in., over-all widths. The dimensions for the 27-in. case, Unit III in the group arrangement, are indicated on the drawing by encircled figures. All other figures are for the 30-in. case, Unit IV. The group arrangement in Plate 25 shows both widths. The unit shown at the right in group A, in Plate 25, is the 30-in. case, with the addition of a 24-in. attached leaf, supported on the right end by a round, detachable post. The extension may be used as a writing table. The lower illustration is the 27-in. width case.

Fig. 70. Playroom storage case.

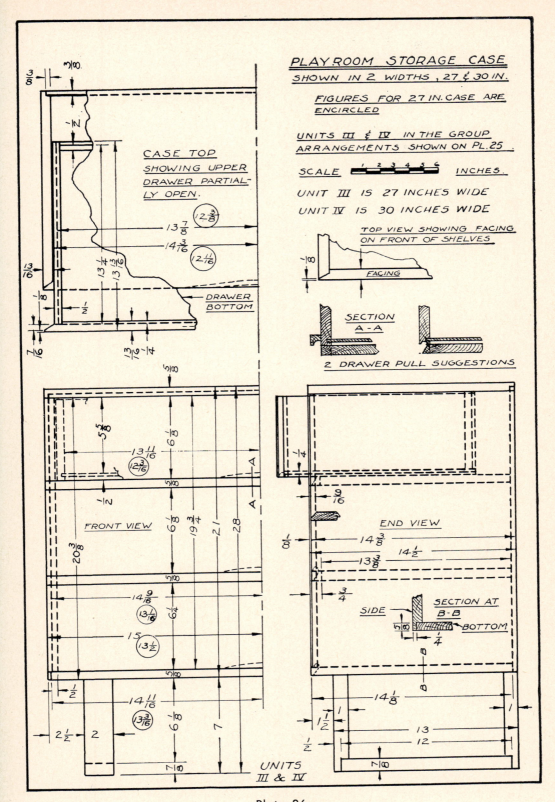

PLAY ROOM STORAGE CASE

SHOWN IN 2 WIDTHS, 27 & 30 IN.

FIGURES FOR 27 IN. CASE ARE
ENCIRCLED

UNITS III & IV IN THE GROUP
ARRANGEMENTS SHOWN ON PL.25.

SCALE [1 2 3 4 5 6] INCHES.

UNIT III IS 27 INCHES WIDE
UNIT IV IS 30 INCHES WIDE

TOP VIEW SHOWING FACING
ON FRONT OF SHELVES

FACING

SECTION
A-A

2 DRAWER PULL SUGGESTIONS

CASE TOP
SHOWING UPPER
DRAWER PARTIAL-
LY OPEN.

DRAWER
BOTTOM

FRONT VIEW

END VIEW

SIDE

SECTION AT
B-B

BOTTOM

UNITS
III & IV

Plate 26.

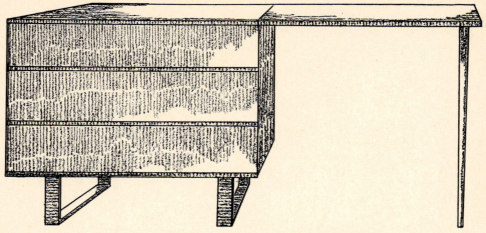

Fig. 71. Writing table attached to storage cases.

Material: Basswood, birch, maple, knotty pine, or oak

Stock sizes: $\frac{5}{8} \times 7\frac{1}{2} \times 20\frac{1}{2}$ ft.; $1 \times 7\frac{1}{2} \times 14\frac{1}{2}$ ft.; $\frac{1}{2} \times 6\frac{1}{2} \times 14$ ft.; $\frac{3}{8} \times 7 \times 8$ ft.; $\frac{3}{16}$ plywood 28×40; $1\frac{1}{4} \times 2 \times 54$

Finish: The case, natural, in oil and wax; the tops natural or painted

PROCEDURE

1. Using the procedures in Chapter 2 make:

   1 top, $\frac{5}{8} \times 14\frac{1}{2} \times 30$, rabbeted $\frac{3}{8} \times \frac{3}{8}$ for back panel

   1 bottom, $\frac{5}{8} \times 14\frac{1}{8} \times 29\frac{3}{8}$

   2 sides, $1\frac{3}{16} \times 14\frac{3}{8} \times 20\frac{3}{8}$, beveled 45 deg. along front edge, and rabbeted $\frac{3}{8} \times \frac{3}{8}$ along the back edge for back panel. Also bored for shelf dowels. Rabbet inside bottom edges $\frac{1}{2} \times \frac{5}{8}$ to fit over bottom board.

   2 shelves, $\frac{5}{8} \times 13\frac{3}{8} \times 28\frac{3}{8}$, bored for dowels

   2 shelf facing strips, $\frac{5}{8} \times \frac{3}{4} \times 30$, mitered at both ends to fit into bevel of sides

   1 back, $\frac{3}{8} \times 20\frac{3}{4} \times 29\frac{1}{8}$

   The above pieces are, with exception of facing strips, built up of two widths of stock, joined, doweled, glued, and then planed to size.

2. 4 base posts, 1 (full inch) $\times 2 \times 7$, cut to lap floor piece $\frac{1}{2}$ in.

   2 floor pieces, $\frac{7}{8} \times 2 \times 12$

   2 drawer fronts, $1 \times 6\frac{1}{8} \times 30$, beveled at both ends, cut along ends to lap drawer sides, and grooved $\frac{3}{16} \times \frac{1}{4}$ for bottom

   1 bottom drawer front, $1 \times 6\frac{1}{4} \times 30$, same as above

   6 drawer sides, $\frac{1}{2} \times 6\frac{1}{8} \times 13\frac{1}{4}$, grooved for bottom

   3 drawer backs, $\frac{1}{2} \times 5\frac{5}{8} \times 27\frac{3}{8}$

   3 drawer bottoms, $\frac{3}{16}$ plywood, $13\frac{1}{4} \times 27\frac{3}{4}$

3. Surface plane and sand all pieces.

4. Drill screw holes for sides and for base into bottom board, and bore dowel holes into the top end of the sides. Bore corresponding holes into underside of the top.

5. Glue and screw bottom to the sides, and glue and dowel the top and the shelves to the sides. Clamp and then nail the panel into the back. Assemble bases with glue and screws from below the floor pieces. Then screw this assembly to the case from the inside of bottom.

6. Attach front shelf facing strips with glue and nails.

7. Nail drawer sides to fronts, and nail backs to sides; insert bottoms and nail.

8. Drawer pulls in keeping with the

Fig. 72. Open-shelf cabinet.

style are inconspicuous. A single wood handle running the length of the drawer, attached to the bottom edge of each, the handle gouged out below for finger holds, is a common method used for pulls. There are no handles visible on the cases in the book. Finger holds are gouged on the underside of the drawer front itself, as shown in Plate 26. To grip these, finger space must be provided on the shelf strip separating the drawers and also on the bottom strip. This may be a 2-in. wide space in the center of the strip. It may also be a beveled area, the shelf strip gradually turning into a long bevel and then turning out again at the other end. The maximum depths of the bevels occur at the area of finger holds.

9. The extended top, pictured in Figure 71, is attached to Unit III, making it into a writing table (Unit IV in the group). It is glued, doweled, and planed to size $\frac{5}{8} \times 14\frac{1}{2} \times 24$ (stock not included in the list), and attached to the right side of Unit III with brass loose pin hinges, to be detached

when not in use. The leg at its right end is a 1-in. birch dowel, provided with a headless bolt, thread end up. The dowel is screwed into a tapped metal plate fixed to the underside of the board.

Open Shelf Cabinet
(SEE PLATE 27 AND FIGURE 72)

Material: Basswood, knotty pine, or cherry

Stock sizes: $1\frac{5}{8} \times 1\frac{5}{8} \times 60$; $1 \times 7 \times 27$ ft.; $\frac{1}{2} \times 7 \times 64$; $\frac{3}{8} \times 8 \times 80$

Finish: Natural, in oil and wax

PROCEDURE

1. Using the directions in Chapter 2, make:
   4 legs, $1\frac{5}{8} \times 1\frac{5}{8} \times 14\frac{1}{8}$, rounded, tapered, and doweled at top end
   1 top, $1 \times 13\frac{1}{4} \times 40$, made up of two widths of stock, joined, doweled, and glued, and then planed to size
   1 bottom, $1 \times 13\frac{1}{4} \times 39\frac{1}{2}$, made of two widths of 7-in. stock
   2 shelves, $1 \times 12\frac{7}{8} \times 39$, made of two widths of 7-in. stock
   2 sides, $\frac{1}{2} \times 13\frac{1}{4} \times 15\frac{7}{16}$, made of two widths of 7-in. stock

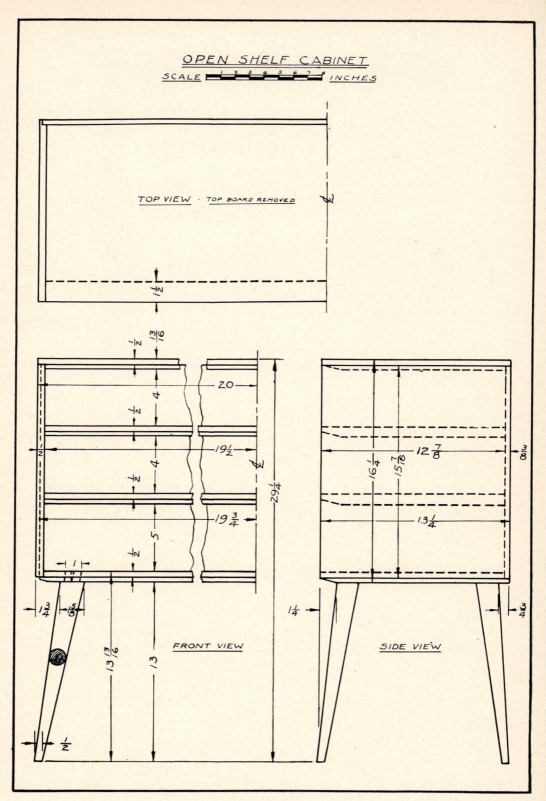

Plate 27.

1 back, $\frac{3}{8} \times 15\frac{7}{16} \times 39\frac{1}{2}$, made of two pieces

2. Cut a rabbet at each end of the top board, $\frac{1}{4} \times \frac{1}{2}$, to lap over the end panels, and $\frac{3}{8} \times \frac{3}{8}$ along the back edge, to receive the back panel, as shown. Do the same to the bottom piece, cutting the end rabbets $\frac{1}{2}$ in. high $\times \frac{1}{4}$ in. wide.

3. Plane a $\frac{5}{16} \times 1\frac{1}{2}$ chamfer on the underside front edge of top, shelves, and bottom, as shown, leaving a $\frac{1}{2}$-in. face on each, the latter running into the line of end rabbet cuts as is indicated in Plate 27. Also chamfer both ends of the bottom on its underside, $\frac{1}{8} \times \frac{3}{8}$.

4. Bore holes into the bottom for leg dowels, as explained in Chapter 1, using a jig similar to that shown in Plate 1, and rotating it so that most of the angle is seen from the front.

5. Surface plane and sand all pieces.

6. Glue and wedge legs as explained, then trim and sand.

7. Glue and nail sides to top and bottom. Add shelves and back. Wipe off surplus glue.

8. Finish all over as explained in Chapter 4.

As the cabinet is designed, it is useful for periodicals, sheet music, or linen.

If the cabinet were given one shelf in place of two, and if the front edge all around were rabbeted and faced as are those in Figure 74, glass sliding doors may be added to make the piece a buffet. Without shelves, it will accommodate record albums set up vertically.

Case With Sliding Wood or Glass Doors

(SEE PLATE 28 AND FIGURES 73 AND 74)

Material: Maple, beech, oak, or magnolia

Stock sizes: $\frac{5}{8} \times 8$ in. $\times 20$ ft.; $\frac{1}{2} \times 7$ in. $\times 6$ ft.; $\frac{3}{8} \times 9$ in. $\times 8$ ft.; $1\frac{1}{2} \times 2\frac{1}{4}$ $\times 46$ in. base; $\frac{3}{8} \times 18$ in. by 4 ft. plywood panel for door; substitute $2 \times 2 \times 22$-in. stock for round legs

Finish: Natural, in lacquer and wax

PROCEDURE

1. Make the following pieces, using procedures discussed in Chapter 2.

1 top, $\frac{5}{8} \times 15\frac{5}{8} \times 36$, rabbeted $\frac{3}{8} \times \frac{1}{2}$ at ends, to fit side panels; rabbeted $\frac{7}{8}$ wide $\times \frac{1}{4}$ deep, along inner front edge for doors; and $\frac{3}{8} \times \frac{3}{8}$ along under rear edge for back panel.

1 bottom, $\frac{5}{8} \times 15\frac{5}{8} \times 35\frac{1}{2}$, rabbeted along inside front and rear edges as on the top. Also drilled for screws to be driven into base from the inside,

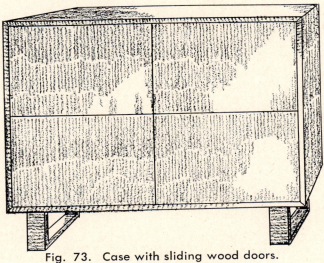

Fig. 73. Case with sliding wood doors.

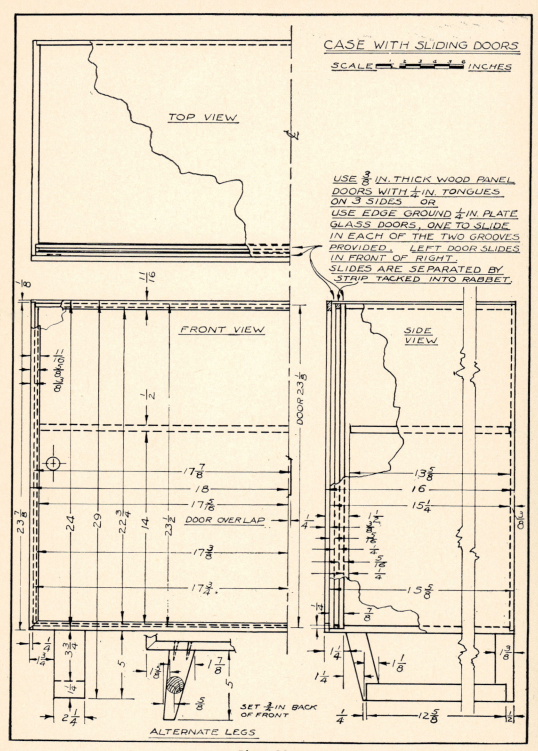

Plate 28.

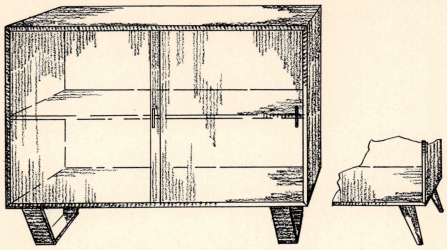

Fig. 74.   Case with sliding glass doors.

and for screws into the sides from underneath.

2 sides, $\frac{5}{8} \times 15\frac{5}{8} \times 23\frac{7}{8}$, rabbeted at top end $\frac{1}{4} \times \frac{1}{2}$, to receive rabbeted end of top, and $\frac{3}{8} \times \frac{5}{8}$ at bottom end to receive bottom. Also rabbeted along rear edges $\frac{3}{8} \times \frac{3}{8}$ for back panel, and $\frac{5}{16} \times \frac{1}{4}$ deep on front edge of left panel for door. The right panel is grooved $\frac{5}{16}$ wide $\times \frac{1}{4}$ deep back of a line $\frac{9}{16}$ in. from the front edge.

2 doors, $\frac{3}{8} \times 17\frac{7}{8} \times 23\frac{1}{8}$ rabbeted on three edges, leaving a $\frac{1}{4} \times \frac{1}{4}$ tongue to slide along top and bottom grooves and fit into side grooves. Finger holes should be cut into the outer ends of each door as shown.

1 shelf, $\frac{1}{2} \times 13\frac{5}{8} \times 34\frac{3}{4}$

1 back, $\frac{3}{8} \times 23\frac{1}{2} \times 35\frac{1}{2}$

2 base pieces, $1\frac{3}{8} \times 2\frac{1}{4} \times 5\frac{1}{4}$, cut to stand at the angle given in detailed drawing and to overlap the floor piece

2 floor pieces, $1\frac{1}{4} \times 2\frac{1}{4} \times 12\frac{5}{8}$

2 back posts, $1\frac{3}{8} \times 2\frac{1}{4} \times 5$, cut to lap floor piece

4 alternate legs, $1\frac{7}{8} \times 1\frac{7}{8} \times 5\frac{1}{4}$, cut to stand at an angle as shown in Plate 28, see Chapter 2.

2 front molding strips, $\frac{3}{8} \times {}^{11}\!/_{16} \times 24$, mitered at both ends

2 front molding strips, $\frac{3}{8} \times {}^{11}\!/_{16} \times 36$, mitered at both ends

2 door slide strips, $\frac{1}{4} \times \frac{1}{4} \times 35$, square at both ends

2. The first six pieces, not including the doors, are made up of two or three widths of stock, joined, doweled, and glued; then planed to the sizes given.

3. Rabbet and groove the above pieces as required.

4. Surface plane all pieces and sand.

5. Glue and clamp sides to top and bottom, and reinforce with screws from the bottom into the sides and with nails from the inside corner into the top. Glue and nail the back into position, and screw and glue the base onto the cabinet. In the case of the frame base, glue and screw into the posts from below before assembly to the case.

6. If alternate legs are used, bore holes and set them according to the directions in the text for Plate 27.

7. Rest shelf on removable pegs, set into shallow holes in the side panels.

8. Fit and set right door into rabbet and nail door slide strips in front of it, leaving a slide space of $\frac{5}{16}$ in. on both the front and the back of the strip. The door should fit into the

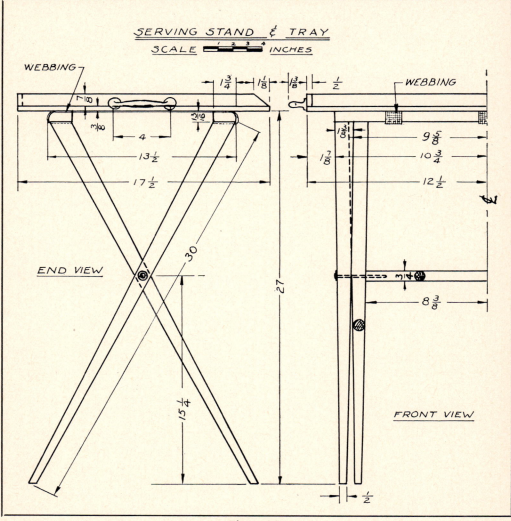

Plate 29.

right-hand groove along the inside edge of the right-side panel. Set the left door and nail the molded facing strips over the front face of the cabinet. Wax the tracks.

9. Finish all over as per directions in Chapter 4.

Figure 74 shows the same cabinet, identical in all details except for the doors which are made of edge ground ¼-in. plate glass. Both doors have a finger hole or a partially ground out finger slot, two thirds of the thickness deep. The glass doors should be 18 × 23⅛ in. each.

Serving Stand and Tray
(SEE PLATE 29 AND FIGURE 75)

Material: Basswood, tulipwood, maple, cherry, or mahogany

Stock sizes: 1½ × 1½ × 10 ft.; 1 × 4 × 22; ⅜ × 7 × 76; 1-in. dowel, 16¾ long; webbing, 35 in.; and two brass handles

Finish: Natural, in oil and wax

PROCEDURE

1. Make four legs for the trestle, using the process described in Chapter 2. Cut them off on both ends at the

angles shown in Plate 29, and drill the center for a 1¼-in. screw.

2. Drill ⁵⁄₃₂-in. hole into the ends of the dowel, and finish the dowel.

3. Plane both edges of the 1-in. wood and make two crossbars for the top of the legs, $1 \times 1\frac{3}{4} \times 21\frac{1}{2}$ in. Round these crossbars on their outer edges, and bevel their inner edges as shown in Plate 29. Drill two screw holes over the position of each leg. See Chapter 3.

4. Assemble the parts of the table with screws and finish all over. Tack three $3 \times 17\frac{1}{2}$ in. bands of colored webbing across the top over the legs.

5. Use the ⅜-in. stock for making the tray:
1 tray bottom, $\frac{3}{8} \times 17\frac{1}{2} \times 25$, made up of three widths, joined, doweled, and glued
1 back edge, $\frac{3}{8} \times \frac{7}{8} \times 24\frac{1}{4}$
2 ends, $\frac{3}{8} \times \frac{7}{8} \times 17\frac{1}{2}$, each cut at 40-deg. angle on front face

6. Surface plane and sand all pieces. Nail back to tray from the underside. Add the sides in the same way.

7. Finish all over, and put on two brass handles as shown in Figure 75.

Fig. 75. Serving stand and tray.

Boy's Study Table With Glass Shelf

(SEE PLATE 30 AND FIGURE 76)

Material: Knotty pine, beech, cherry, or tulipwood

Stock sizes: 4 pieces leg stock, $1\frac{1}{2} \times 1\frac{1}{2}$

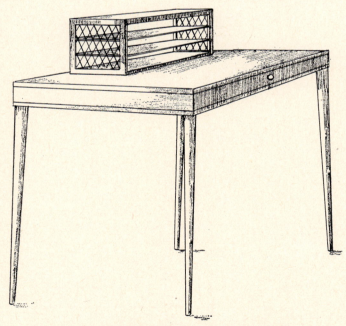

Fig. 76. Study table with glass shelves.

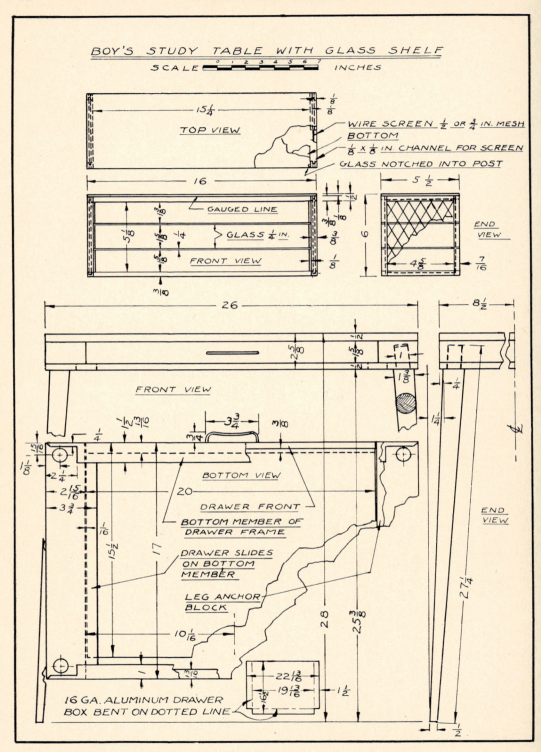

BOY'S STUDY TABLE WITH GLASS SHELF

Plate 30.

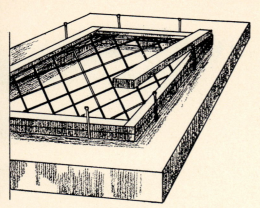

Fig. 77. Method of gluing frames on a work board.

× 27½; 1 piece each, 2 × 6 × 17½; 1× 4 × 21; ½ × 8 × 8¼ ft.

Finish: Natural, in lacquer and wax

PROCEDURE

1. Make legs according to directions in Chapter 2.
2. Plane both edges of remaining pieces of wood and present the following pieces:
   1 top, ½ × 17 × 26, made of three widths of stock, glued and doweled
   2 side blocks, 1⅝ × 2¹⁵⁄₁₆ × 17, drilled for screws
   1 back panel, 1 × 1⅝ × 20⅛, drilled for screws
   2 side bottom pieces, ½ × 3¾ × 17, cut to fit front and back strips, as shown in Plate 30
   1 front strip below drawer, ½ × 1½ × 26, cut to lap sidepieces
   1 back strip below panel, ½ × 1 × 26, cut to lap sidepieces, both front and back strips mitered at corners
   1 drawer front, 1 × 1⅝ × 20, rabbeted ³⁄₃₂ × ⅜ on bottom and sides to accommodate aluminum drawer box
   1 metal box for drawer, 16 ga. × 16½ × 22¹³⁄₁₆ sheet aluminum
3. Screw side blocks and back panel to the underside of the top and nail under them the bottom strips, sides, front, and back. Place screws and nails into the sidepieces with a view to strengthening the area around the legs.
4. Bore holes for legs as described in Chapter 1. Glue legs into their respective sockets.
5. Lay out a blank for the drawer box as shown in the sketch at the bottom of Plate 30. Cut out the two corner pieces, and clamp the metal between two hardwood blocks and bend the side and two end flaps at right angles to the bottom. The bending may be done by hammering against a third block of wood until the metal bends are sharp.

   Fasten metal box to drawer front with nails. File off rough corners of metal and emery all edges.
6. Finish table all over. See Chapter 4.
7. Add a drawer handle of contemporary design, as shown.

Glass Shelf for Boy's Desk
(SEE PLATE 30 AND FIGURE 77)

Material: Same as for table shown in Figure 76

Stock sizes: ⅜ × 2 × 25; ⅜ × 6 × 16½; ½ × 6 × 16½; 2 glass shelves, 5½ × 15¼, ground front and sides; 2 wire screens, ⅛ × 4⅞ × 5⅜, made of standard metal lath, or preferably of 16-ga. annealed copper wire, woven around nails on a work board, soldered, polished, cut, and lacquered

Finish: Natural, in lacquer and wax

PROCEDURE

1. Plane back and front surfaces and both long edges of the first piece of stock and gauge ⅛ in. all around the edges from both faces. Rip between lines and plane to lines. Then, as described in Chapter 2, prepare the following pieces:
   8 pcs. ⅛ × ⁷⁄₁₆ × 5¹³⁄₁₆, posts
   8 pcs. ⅛ × ⅜ × 4⅝, top and bottom of frame

Fig. 78. Hobby table with shelves.

4 inside post strips, $\frac{1}{8} \times \frac{5}{16} \times 5\frac{13}{16}$

4 inside top and bottom strips, $\frac{1}{8} \times \frac{1}{4} \times 4\frac{7}{8}$

4 strips, $\frac{1}{8} \times \frac{1}{4} \times 5\frac{1}{16}$, rounded on one side

2. Also, make 1 top, $\frac{1}{2} \times 5\frac{1}{2} \times 16$, rabbeted $\frac{3}{8} \times \frac{3}{8}$ at both ends to fit over end frames, and gauged along front face to simulate a wood joint at the level of the rabbet.

1 bottom, $\frac{3}{8} \times 5\frac{1}{2} \times 15\frac{1}{4}$.

3. Glue frames together on a work board, using nails to hold pieces in place, as shown in Figure 77. Proceed as follows: Lay down a frame of strips; two post pieces, $\frac{1}{8} \times \frac{7}{16} \times 5\frac{13}{16}$, and two crosspieces, $\frac{1}{8} \times \frac{3}{8} \times 4\frac{5}{8}$ laid inside the posts. Over these glue two vertical strips, $\frac{1}{8} \times \frac{5}{16} \times 5\frac{13}{16}$, and over the crosspieces glue two

$\frac{1}{8} \times \frac{1}{4} \times 4\frac{7}{8}$ strips. Wipe off the surplus glue and set the metal screens into the frames. Glue the outer posts and the crosspieces to the front face of the frame. Clamp frames and wipe off the glue. Allow two hours for drying.

4. Clean up and sand frames. Surface plane and sand top and bottom. Glue and nail top and bottom to frames, using three No. $18 \times \frac{7}{8}$ brads to the joint.

5. Glue the remaining $\frac{1}{8} \times \frac{1}{4} \times 5\frac{1}{16}$ strips to the inside of the posts, with rounded side toward inside of case. When dry, notch these through to the frame, adjusting width of notch to the thickness of the glass.

6. Finish all over as in Chapter 4, and slide glass shelves into place.

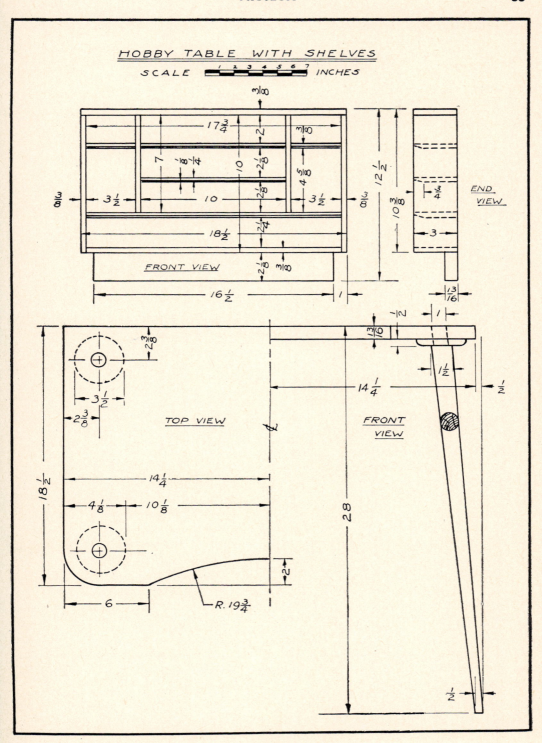

HOBBY TABLE WITH SHELVES

Plate 31.

Hobby Table

(SEE PLATE 31 AND FIGURE 78)

Material: Basswood, knotty pine, tulip-wood, or cherry

Stock sizes: $1 \times 10 \times 58$; $\frac{1}{2} \times 3\frac{1}{2} \times 14$; $1\frac{1}{2} \times 1\frac{1}{2} \times 10$ ft.

Finish: Natural, in oil and wax

PROCEDURE

1. Cut the first piece of stock into two lengths, join the pieces, dowel, and glue. When the glue has set, square the board as described in Chapter 2. Mark out the contour on the top and saw to shape as shown in Plate 31. Then surface plane, and sand.

2. Cut out four $3\frac{1}{2}$ by $\frac{1}{2}$-in. disks. Round the edges on one face of each, and drill screw holes. Fasten these to the underside of the top with glue and screws as shown. Bore holes for legs as described in Chapter 1.

3. Make four legs as described in Chapter 2, and glue, wedge, and trim them.

4. Finish the table all over as described in Chapter 4.

Shelves for Hobby Table

(SEE PLATE 31 AND FIGURE 78)

Material and Finish: Same as for table

Stock sizes: $\frac{3}{8} \times 6\frac{1}{2} \times 50$; $\frac{1}{2} \times 3\frac{1}{2} \times 19$; $1 \times 2\frac{1}{2} \times 17$

PROCEDURE

1. Plane both edges of first piece and one on each of the others. Make the pieces described below.
   2 shelves, $\frac{3}{8} \times 3 \times 17\frac{3}{4}$
   2 sides, $\frac{3}{8} \times 3 \times 9\frac{7}{8}$
   2 shelves, $\frac{3}{8} \times 3 \times 10$
   2 partitions, $\frac{3}{8} \times 3 \times 7$
   2 shelves, $\frac{3}{8} \times 3 \times 3\frac{1}{2}$
   1 top, $\frac{1}{2} \times 3 \times 18\frac{1}{2}$
   1 base, $1\frac{3}{16} \times 2\frac{1}{8} \times 16\frac{1}{2}$

2. Chamfer all shelves, but the bottom one, $\frac{1}{8} \times \frac{3}{4}$ in. on the underside, as shown.

3. Surface plane and sand all pieces.

4. Nail the 10-in. shelves to the partitions, and then nail the long shelf to the partitions. Next nail this assembly and the lower shelf to the outer sides. After that add the top and the short shelves, nailing the latter first from the outside and then fasten them with nails set at an angle from beneath the middle shelf.

5. Finish all over as explained in Chapter 4.

6. Hang the shelf on the wall, the base just touching the table.

Contemporary Desk

(SEE PLATE 32 AND FIGURE 79)

Material: Basswood, knotty pine, maple, or oak

Stock sizes: 1×7 in. $\times 31$ ft.; $1 \times 8 \times 84$ in.; $1\frac{1}{2} \times 5 \times 14$; $\frac{1}{2} \times 11 \times 70$; $\frac{3}{8} \times 8 \times 48$; $\frac{1}{4} \times 13\frac{3}{8} \times 37$ plywood

Finish: Natural, in oil or lacquer and wax

PROCEDURE

1. Make the following parts:
   1 top, $1 \times 22\frac{1}{2} \times 50$, using three widths of stock, doweled, glued, cut to size, and then cut to contour
   2 sides, $1 \times 20 \times 23\frac{11}{16}$, made of three widths of stock, rabbeted $\frac{9}{16} \times \frac{13}{16}$ to lap bottom board, and rabbeted $\frac{3}{8} \times \frac{3}{8}$ for backboard
   1 right end board, $1 \times 11 \times 28\frac{3}{16}$, made of two widths of stock, glued, doweled, and cut to size
   1 facing on the above, $1 \times 1\frac{1}{4} \times 23\frac{11}{16}$, glued to front face of right end
   2 rails, $1 \times 2 \times 25\frac{3}{16}$, bored for dowels to join with case and right end board, and drilled and countersunk to be screwed to the top from beneath
   1 bottom of case, $1 \times 19\frac{1}{4} \times 15$, drilled and countersunk from below to fasten to sideboards, and from above to fasten to the 2 base posts
   2 shelves, $1 \times 19\frac{1}{4} \times 13\frac{7}{8}$, bored for

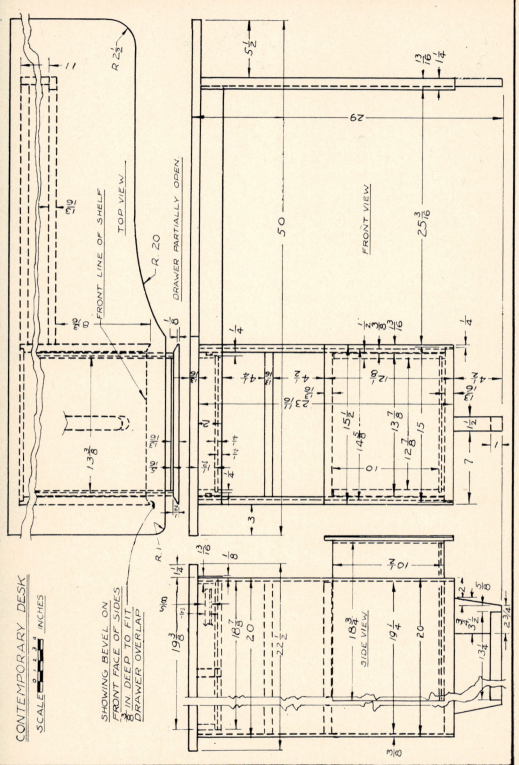

CONTEMPORARY DESK

SCALE INCHES

SHOWING BEVEL ON
FRONT FACE OF SIDES
⅜ IN. DEEP TO FIT
DRAWER OVERLAP

FRONT LINE OF SHELF

TOP VIEW

DRAWER PARTIALLY OPEN.

FRONT VIEW

SIDE VIEW

Plate 32.

Fig. 79. Contemporary desk.

dowels to fasten into sides
1 back, $\frac{3}{8} \times 14\frac{5}{8} \times 23\frac{11}{16}$, glued up and planed to size
2 base uprights, $1\frac{1}{2} \times 3\frac{1}{2} \times 4\frac{1}{2}$, lapped to fit over floor piece. The lap is $2\frac{1}{8} \times 1$ in. Taper the front face from $3\frac{1}{2}$ in. at the top to $2\frac{3}{4}$ in. below. Round off the edge as shown.
1 base floor piece, $1\frac{1}{2} \times 1 \times 13\frac{1}{4}$, drilled and countersunk from below to fasten to base posts
1 lower drawer front, $1 \times 12\frac{1}{8} \times 15\frac{1}{2}$, rabbeted $1\frac{5}{16} \times \frac{5}{16}$, on both sides to fit over drawer sides, and grooved $\frac{1}{4} \times \frac{1}{4}$ above a line $1\frac{1}{16}$ in. from the inside bottom to fit drawer bottom. $1\frac{3}{16}$ in. of the rabbeted sides are beveled to fit against the beveled case sides, the outer edge of the bevel being left blunt.
1 upper drawer front, $1 \times 2 \times 15\frac{1}{2}$, cut same as the above except for the groove at the bottom which is cut $\frac{1}{4}$ in. above the bottom edge
2 lower drawer sides, $\frac{1}{2} \times 10\frac{1}{2} \times$ $18\frac{3}{4}$, grooved for drawer bottom
2 upper drawer sides, $\frac{1}{2} \times 2 \times 18\frac{3}{4}$, grooved as above, and grooved $\frac{5}{16}$ in. deep $\times \frac{5}{8}$ on outside faces to slide over runners
1 lower drawer back, $\frac{1}{2} \times 10 \times 12\frac{7}{8}$
1 upper drawer back, $\frac{1}{2} \times 1\frac{1}{2} \times 12\frac{7}{8}$
2 drawer bottoms, $\frac{1}{4}$ plywood $\times 13\frac{3}{8}$ $\times 18\frac{1}{2}$
2 upper drawer runners, $\frac{1}{4} \times \frac{1}{2} \times$ 18, drilled for screws

2. Surface plane and sand all pieces
3. Bore dowel holes into right side of case and into the right end post to correspond with dowel holes bored into rails.
4. Bore dowel holes into case sides to correspond with those bored into the shelves.
5. Bevel front faces of case sides inward to a depth of $\frac{3}{8}$ in., to fit against the bevel of the drawer sides. Shelves and bottom fit up to the $\frac{3}{8}$-in. bevel.
6. Assemble bottom of case to sides with glue and screws. At the same time,

Fig. 80. Desk with letter file.

fasten shelves with glue and dowels.

7. Clamp the case and bore $\frac{3}{8}$-in. dowel holes into the top edges to fit into corresponding holes bored into the underside of the top; then glue and clamp the case to the top. Nail through the joint from the case into the top to reinforce the joint, driving the brads at an angle.

8. Glue, dowel, and clamp rails into case and right end, and screw the rails into the table top from beneath.

9. Assemble floor piece to base posts with glue and screws, and fasten this assembly to the case from the inside.

10. Screw upper drawer runners to the case.

11. Nail backboard to the case.

12. Assemble drawer sides to fronts, and sides to backs. Insert bottoms and nail. Cut grooves for finger holds on the underside of the drawer fronts.

13. Finish the desk all over as explained in Chapter 4.

Desk With Letter File
(SEE PLATE 33 AND FIGURE 80)

Material: Basswood, knotty pine, clear maple, or oak

Stock sizes: 1×7 in. $\times 33$ ft.; 1×8 in. $\times 10$ ft.; $1\frac{1}{2} \times 8 \times 27$; $\frac{1}{4}$-in. plywood $15\frac{1}{8} \times 19\frac{5}{16}$ (1 in., mentioned below, is the standard $\frac{3}{16}$ in. dimension)

Finish: Natural, in oil or lacquer and wax

PROCEDURE

1. Make the listed pieces, using the procedure outlined in Chapter 2.

   1 top, $1 \times 22 \times 45\frac{1}{2}$, glued and doweled, using three widths of stock; rabbeted all around $\frac{1}{4} \times \frac{9}{16}$, to accommodate the rabbeted apron

   2 apron pieces, $1 \times 1\frac{7}{8} \times 45\frac{1}{2}$, rabbeted $\frac{9}{16} \times \frac{9}{16}$ on inside edge to fit into top rabbet, and mitered at both ends

   2 apron pieces, $1 \times 1\frac{7}{8} \times 22$, cut as above. The right apron is lapped $\frac{3}{8}$

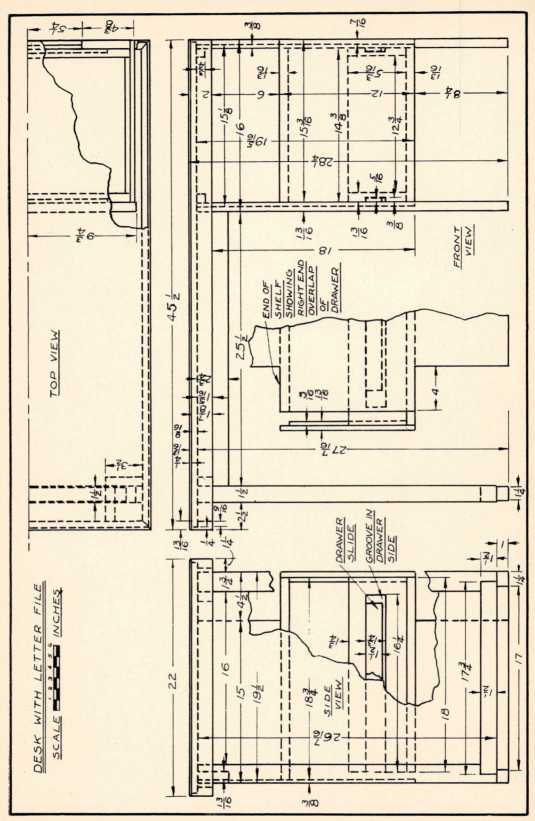

DESK WITH LETTER FILE

SCALE 1 2 3 4 5 6 INCHES

TOP VIEW

FRONT VIEW

SIDE VIEW

END OF SHELF SHOWING RIGHT END OVERLAP OF DRAWER

DRAWER SLIDE

GROOVE IN DRAWER SIDE

Plate 33.

in. deep, 15 in. long to fit the joint of the right end upright

2 posts, $1\frac{1}{2} \times 1\frac{3}{4} \times 26\frac{7}{16}$, lapped below to fit over the lower crosspiece, the cut measuring $\frac{7}{8} \times 1\frac{1}{2}$

1 lower crosspiece, $1\frac{1}{2} \times 1\frac{1}{2} \times 17\frac{3}{4}$, drilled and countersunk at each end to fasten to the posts from below

1 floor piece, $1 \times 1\frac{1}{4} \times 17$, drilled and countersunk in three places to fasten into the lower crosspiece from below, as described in Chapter 3

1 back rail, $1 \times 2\frac{3}{4} \times 25\frac{1}{2}$, bored at one end for dowels, and drilled and countersunk in three places to be fastened to the top

1 center partition, $1 \times 19\frac{1}{2} \times 27\frac{7}{16}$, rabbeted on the back edge $\frac{3}{8} \times \frac{1}{4}$ to hold plywood back down to bottom of drawer, and then bored for dowels on the shelf level

1 right endpiece, $1 \times 15 \times 27\frac{7}{16}$, bored and rabbeted as above. Rabbet the top outer edge, $\frac{7}{16} \times 1\frac{5}{16}$ to lap the apron

1 plywood back panel, $\frac{1}{4} \times 15\frac{1}{8} \times 19\frac{5}{16}$

2 fastening strips, $\frac{3}{4} \times \frac{3}{4} \times 15$, drilled and countersunk on two sides to fasten partition and end to top

1 shelf, $1 \times 18\frac{3}{4} \times 14\frac{3}{8}$, bored for dowels to fit into partition and endpiece holes

1 drawer front, $1 \times 12 \times 15\frac{3}{16}$, rabbeted $\frac{5}{16} \times 1\frac{3}{16}$ on the top, bottom, and left side, and $\frac{5}{16} \times 1\frac{5}{8}$ on the right side

2 drawer sides, $1 \times 5\frac{3}{16} \times 18$, grooved $\frac{3}{8} \times 1\frac{3}{4}$ on outside faces to fit over runners (groove terminates $1\frac{1}{2}$ in. from front)

1 drawer bottom, $1 \times 14\frac{3}{8} \times 18$

1 drawer back, $1 \times 5\frac{3}{16} \times 12\frac{3}{4}$

1 drawer right face, $1 \times 4 \times 12$, to be added by dowel and glue to right side at drawer level

2 drawer slides, $\frac{5}{16} \times 1\frac{1}{2} \times 16\frac{1}{4}$, drilled and countersunk

2 front leg anchor blocks, $1 \times 1\frac{5}{16} \times 3\frac{1}{2}$, drilled and countersunk

2. Surface plane and sand all pieces.

3. Glue apron to top and reinforce it from the inside with brads.

4. Glue and screw lower crosspiece into the lap joints of the posts, and round the lower post corners. Add the floor piece with screws from below.

5. Glue and screw anchor blocks to the top of the front post. These fasten to two adjacent sides.

6. Bore dowel holes for rail into back post, and glue and clamp rail to post. Drill, countersink screw holes into case for rail joint, and drill corresponding holes into right end of rail.

7. Glue and screw front post to underside of table top through the anchor pieces, and screw the rail to the top.

8. Block up space between front post and apron with wood and glue.

9. Glue and screw fastening strips to the top edges of partition and right endpieces, setting them $\frac{1}{8}$ in. under the edge. Glue and dowel the shelf between the partition and right end. Glue and screw this assembly to the underside of the top. Glue and screw rail to case and nail plywood panel into the back rabbet.

10. Screw drawer runners to the inside walls of the case, aligning the top of the drawer front with the top line of the shelf.

11. Nail and glue the drawer sides into the rabbet of the front, and add the bottom and back.

12. Glue and dowel the right face to the side of the drawer to close the space left unfinished because of the narrowed right end upright.

13. Finish all over as explained in Chapter 4.

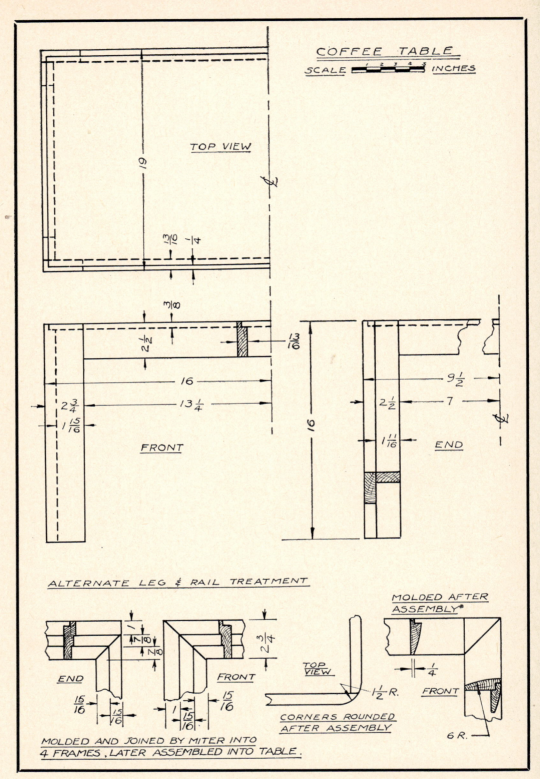

COFFEE TABLE

SCALE 1 2 3 4 5 INCHES

TOP VIEW

$\frac{13}{16}$ $\frac{1}{4}$

19

$\frac{3}{8}$

$2\frac{1}{2}$ $\frac{13}{16}$

16

$13\frac{1}{4}$

$2\frac{3}{4}$

$1\frac{15}{16}$

FRONT

16

$9\frac{1}{2}$

$2\frac{1}{2}$ 7

$1\frac{11}{16}$

END

ALTERNATE LEG & RAIL TREATMENT

MOLDED AFTER ASSEMBLY*

$\frac{7}{8}$

$\frac{7}{8}$

$2\frac{3}{4}$

END

$\frac{15}{16}$ $\frac{15}{16}$

FRONT

1 $\frac{15}{16}$ $\frac{15}{16}$

TOP VIEW

$1\frac{1}{2}$ R.

CORNERS ROUNDED AFTER ASSEMBLY

$\frac{1}{4}$

FRONT

6 R.

MOLDED AND JOINED BY MITER INTO
4 FRAMES, LATER ASSEMBLED INTO TABLE.

Plate 34.

Fig. 81. Coffee table.

Coffee Table

(SEE PLATE 34 AND FIGURE 81)

Materials: Basswood, knotty pine, cherry, mahogany, maple, or oak

Stock sizes: $\frac{3}{8} \times 7 \times 95$; $1 \times 5 \times 108$

Finish: Natural, in lacquer and wax

PROCEDURE

1. Make the following pieces, as directed in Chapter 2:
   1 top, $\frac{3}{8} \times 18\frac{1}{2} \times 31\frac{1}{2}$, glued and doweled, using three widths of stock. See Chapter 3.
   4 leg pieces, $1 \times 1\frac{11}{16} \times 16$
   4 leg pieces, $1 \times 2\frac{3}{4} \times 16$
   2 rails, $1 \times 2\frac{1}{2} \times 14$, rabbeted $\frac{3}{8} \times \frac{9}{16}$ to fit top
   2 rails, $1 \times 2\frac{1}{2} \times 26\frac{1}{2}$, rabbeted as above
2. Surface plane and sand all pieces.

Glue the narrow leg pieces to the wide pieces as shown. When the glue has set, plane the legs and sand.
3. Mark and bore holes for dowels.
4. Set the parts together temporarily and mark legs for top rabbet. Disassemble and cut with saw and chisel.
5. Glue and clamp the rails to the legs. Fit the top and fasten it into the table by means of screws through fastening blocks from below. See Chapter 3.
6. Finish all over as explained in Chapter 4.

Below the coffee table shown in Plate 34 are sketches of alternate designs for legs and rails, using the same general construction. In the first of these sketches, the leg and rail joints are mitered and doweled into four separate frames, each constituting a complete side. When the glue in these is dry, they are glued and

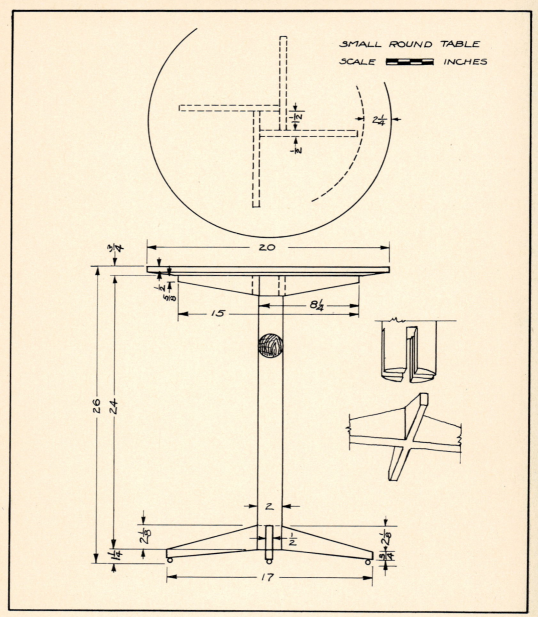

Plate 35.

doweled together into a table. The moldings shown are cut prior to the joining.

In the second of the sketches, the table is assembled as in Figure 81. The rabbeting of the leg tops is left until after the rounding of the legs. The rabbet is then continued around the bend at each corner.

In the third sketch, the table is assembled as was done in making the table already described. Legs and rails of each side are marked and worked down, rounding inward as shown. The rounding of the sides and rails meet in a sharp 45-deg. corner.

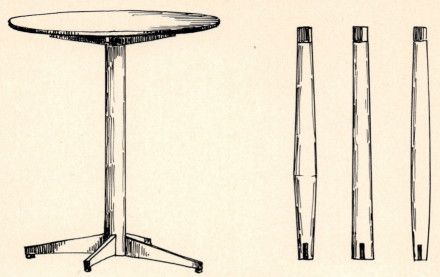

Fig. 82. Small round lamp table.

Small Round Lamp Table

(SEE PLATE 35 AND FIGURE 82)

Material: Mahogany, walnut, maple, or korena wood

Stock sizes: $1 \times 7 \times 84$. This includes wood for built-up post. Also $\frac{1}{2} \times 3\frac{1}{2} \times 50$

Finish: Natural, in oil and wax

PROCEDURE

1. Make the following pieces according to the directions given in Chapter 2. 1 top, $1 \times 20 \times 20$, glued, doweled, cut, and finished to size, using three widths of stock. See Chapter 3. Chamfer the bottom side of the top piece to reduce the face edge to $\frac{1}{2}$-in. thickness all around.

2. Make the post, which is shown in the drawing to be straight. Vary the shape of the post if desired. For example, taper it from a point 4 in. up to a top reduced to $1\frac{3}{4}$ in. in diameter; or taper it both ways from a point 10 in. up, reducing the botton to $1\frac{7}{8}$ in. and the top, $1\frac{3}{4}$ in. Make the taper either straight or barrel shaped.
   In making the post, glue three 2×24-in. rough pieces, face to face, and, when set, square the post and shape it round.
   Square $1\frac{3}{4}$ in. of the top end as shown in the drawing, to receive the brackets on which the top is secured; and cut cross grooves at the lower end to take the cross-lapped feet. This joint should be accurately cut to be tight.

3. Make two foot pieces out of $\frac{1}{2}$-in. stock, and assemble them by cross-lap joining. They should then be glued into the close-fitting grooves in the post. Terminate the outer ends with brass cups, and add a wood pad, disk, or ball below to raise the feet off the floor.

4. Make four bracket pieces out of the remaining $\frac{1}{2}$-in. stock, drill them for screws, and glue and screw them to the squared end of the post, just under the top. Drill these for screws, and secure them to the top from underneath.

5. Sand the table and apply one coat of boiled oil. After 48 hours, rub to a glass-smooth finish all over. Add three coats of car wax, or not, as preferred.

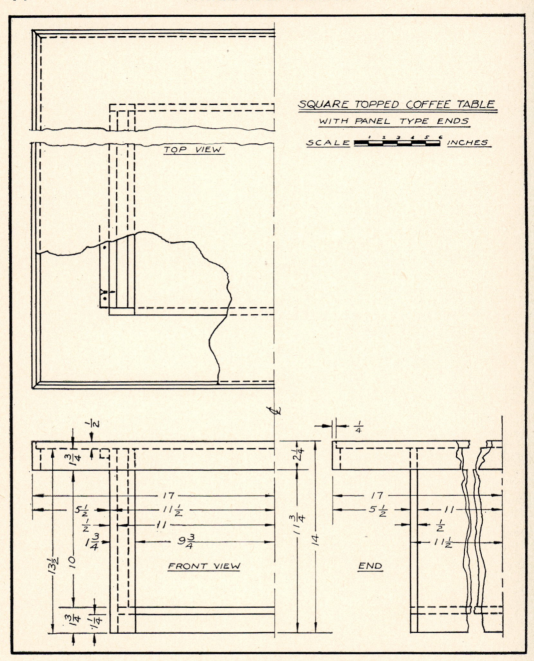

TOP VIEW

SQUARE TOPPED COFFEE TABLE
WITH PANEL TYPE ENDS
SCALE — INCHES

FRONT VIEW   END

Plate 36.

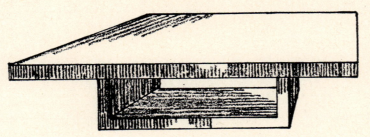

Fig. 83. Square-topped coffee table.

Panel-Type Square-Topped Coffee Table

(SEE PLATE 36 AND FIGURE 83)

Material: Basswood, knotty pine, tulip-wood, maple, or oak

Stock size: ½ in. × 8 in. × 35 ft.

Finish: Natural, in lacquer and wax

PROCEDURE

1. Referring to the directions in Chapter 2, make the following pieces:
   1 top, ½ × 33½ × 33½, made up of five pieces, joined, doweled, glued, and then planed to size
   4 apron pieces, ½ × 2¼ × 34, mitered at each end, and rabbeted ½ × ¼ to receive the top
   2 side panels, ½ × 22 × 13½, grain running vertically
   2 inside panels, ½ × 22 × 11¾, grain running vertically
   1 bottom, ½ × 23 × 22, cut to fit around corner posts
   4 columns, ½ × 1¾ × 13½
   2 base strips, ½ × 1¼ × 19½, drilled to be fastened with screws into the bottom from below
   2 assembly strips, ¾ × ¾ × 22, drilled at intervals of 5 in. for screws

2. Surface plane and sand all pieces.
3. Fasten aprons to the top with glue and nails. Attach columns to both inside and outside panels. Fasten assembly strips to the top of the latter with glue and screws. Fit and nail the bottom to the inside panel, and nail it also to the outside panel and column from underneath. Screw base strips to bottom. Then fasten the lower assembly to the top through assembly strips.
4. Finish all over. Chapter 4.

When top dimensions of any of the tables in this series are altered, change all proportions in the same ratio. If heights from the floor are changed, use leg and rail dimensions of the same cubic content as those from which the change issues. Examples of typical variations in dimensions are given in the text for Plate 41.

A craftsman should be free to change his dimensions to his needs if he considers proportions on the above basis. He may also interchange leg types and detail of the same style, if he is familiar with the style. Familiarity is a matter of association, i.e., of paging through source material until familiar with it. See Introduction.

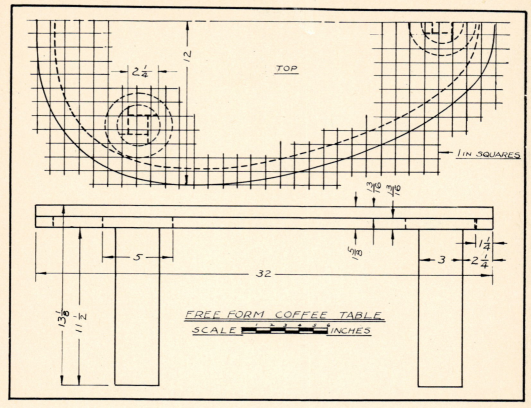

TOP

1 IN SQUARES

FREE FORM COFFEE TABLE
SCALE | 1   2   3   4   5   6 | INCHES

Plate 37.

Free-Form Coffee Table

(SEE PLATE 37 AND FIGURE 84)

Material and Finish: Same as for the previous table

Stock sizes: 1 in. × 10 in. × 15 ft.

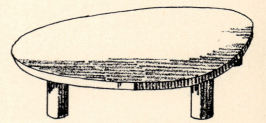

Fig. 84. Free-form coffee table.

PROCEDURE

1. Using the methods described in Chapter 2 make the following:
   1 top, 1 × 24 × 32, using three widths of stock 36 in. long, joined, doweled, glued, and cut to pattern
   12 leg pieces, 1 × 2¼ × 11½
   3 assembly pieces, 1 × 5-in. diameter, drilled for screws, as shown in Plate 39
   1 apron, 1 × 1¼, following the circumference underneath the top
2. The top is marked out just so far from one edge and both ends of glued stock as will allow for the cutting of

apron pieces in the waste immediately outside the cut. This insures similar grain in both top and apron, and there will be few joints in the latter if the work is laid out carefully. If apron widths given cannot be maintained, sacrifice uniformity of width to outside table edge appearance. Cut apron approximately, drill, glue, and screw to the underside of the top. Then trim to the curvature of the top.

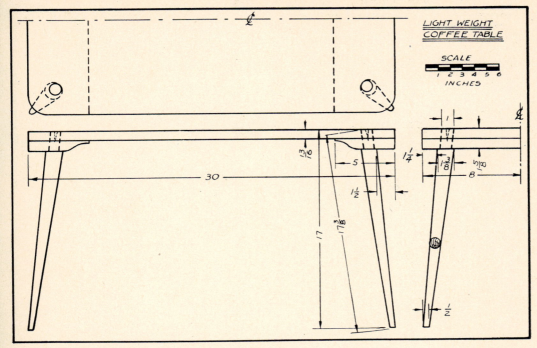

Plate 38.

3. Glue leg pieces, two at a time. When set, glue one unit to another to make three hollow posts. Round these as directed in Chapter 2. Attach them to the circular assembly pieces with glue and screws. Surface plane and finish the top, and assemble the legs.
4. Finish the table all over as per Chapter 4.

Lightweight Coffee Table
(SEE PLATE 38 AND FIGURE 85)
Material and finish: As before

Stock sizes: 1½ in. × 1½ in. × 70 in.; 1 in. × 6 in. × 10½ ft.

PROCEDURE
1. Make the following pieces, using directions in Chapter 2:
   4 legs, 1⅜ × 1⅜ × 17⅜, rounded and tapered from 1⅜ to ½-in. diameter, as explained in Chapter 2
   1 top, 1 × 16 × 30, made up of three widths of stock, joined, doweled, glued, and planed to size

Fig. 85. Lightweight coffee table.

2 leg socket pieces, 1 × 5 × 16 in., drilled for screws, and chamfered on inside edges, ⅝ × 1⅞
2. Surface plane and sand top and socket pieces.
3. Glue and screw socket pieces to underside of the top. Work outer edges of chamfers to ogee curves, as illustrated. Round all four corners, and trim and sand outer faces smooth.
4. Bore leg sockets as explained in Chap-

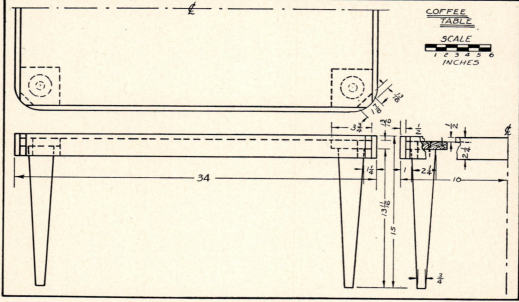

Plate 39.

ter 1, and insert the legs, wedge them, and trim them. See Chapter 2. Finish all over as described in Chapter 4.

Coffee Table

(SEE PLATE 39 AND FIGURE 86)

Material and finish: Same as for previous tables

Stock sizes: $2\frac{1}{4} \times 2\frac{1}{4} \times 60$ in.; $1 \times 4 \times 16\frac{1}{2}$ in.; $\frac{1}{2}$ in. $\times 10$ in. $\times 9$ ft.

PROCEDURE

1. Following the directions in Chapter 2, prepare the following pieces:

4 legs, $2\frac{1}{4} \times 2\frac{1}{4} \times 13\frac{11}{16}$, each leg glued up of three 1-in. pieces, then rounded and tapered

4 leg assembly blocks, $1 \times 3\frac{3}{4} \times 3\frac{3}{4}$ in., drilled for screws, and cut off on one corner to fit against apron insert. See sketch, Plate 39.

1 top, $\frac{1}{2} \times 19 \times 33$

2 aprons, $\frac{1}{2} \times 2\frac{1}{4} \times 19$

2 aprons, $\frac{1}{2} \times 2\frac{1}{4} \times 33$

4 inserts, $1 \times 1\frac{3}{4} \times 1\frac{7}{8}$, cut into tri-

angles to fit into apron corner in order to fill gap made in rounding

2. Surface plane and sand top and aprons. Glue and nail the aprons to the top. Glue and clamp triangular inserts. Then glue and screw leg blocks to legs.

3. Round table corners, and then file and sand. Attach legs with glue and screws.

4. Finish all over as directed in Chapter 4.

Fig. 86. Coffee table.

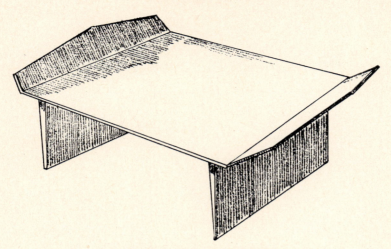

Fig. 87. Low serving table.

Low Serving Table

(SEE PLATE 40 AND FIGURE 87)

Material: Basswood, pine, tulipwood, cherry, mahogany, maple, or oak

Stock size: ½ in. × 7½ in. × 17 ft.

Finish: Natural, using lacquer or oil, and wax

PROCEDURE

1. Make the following pieces:

    1 top, ½ × 21 × 33, made up of three widths of stock, joined, doweled, glued, planed, then beveled on ends to join end leaves

    2 end leaves, ½ × 21 × 3½, joined, doweled, and glued up of three widths of stock, and beveled on one side to join top

    2 end panels, ½ × 18 × 9½, grain running vertically; panels made of three widths of stock

    4 columns, ½ × 1¼ × 9½, tapered to ½ in. at bottom

    2 stretchers, ½ × 1¾ × 26, cut to shape shown

    2 assembly strips, ¾ × ¾ × 18, drilled for four screws on each side

2. Surface plane and sand all pieces.

3. Dowel and glue the end leaves to the top. Screw and glue the assembly strips to the top of the panel. Nail and glue the columns to the panel. Glue and screw stretchers to the panels. Then screw this assembly to the top through the assembly strips and stretchers.

4. Finish all over.

Serving Tables With Metal Legs

(SEE PLATE 40 AND FIGURES 88 AND 89)

Material: Wood, same as for previous table. Chromium-plated steel or polished aluminum tubing

Stock sizes: For the first table, ½ × 7 × 10½ ft.; for the second table, ½ × 7 × 21 ft.; tubing as listed below

Finish: Natural, using lacquer or oil, and wax

Fig. 88.
Pipe legs on
serving table.

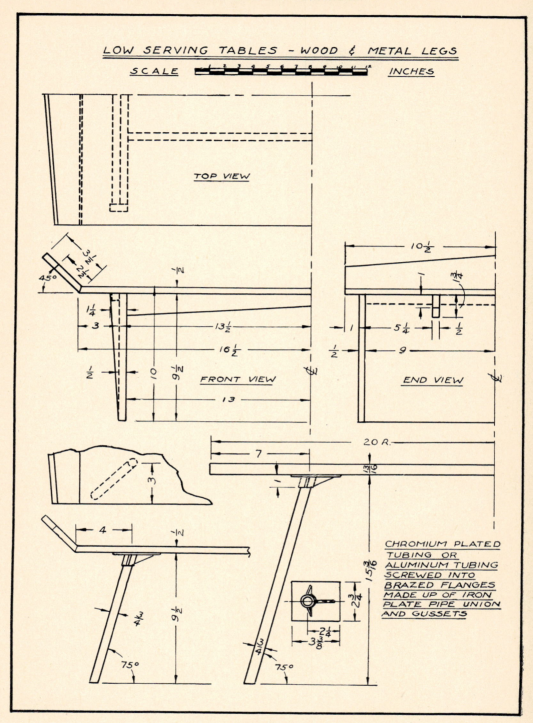

LOW SERVING TABLES – WOOD & METAL LEGS

SCALE   INCHES

TOP VIEW

FRONT VIEW

END VIEW

CHROMIUM PLATED
TUBING OR
ALUMINUM TUBING
SCREWED INTO
BRAZED FLANGES
MADE UP OF IRON
PLATE PIPE UNION
AND GUSSETS

Plate 40.

Fig. 89. Circular serving table with aluminum or
steel pipe legs.

PROCEDURE

1. For making the top of the first table, follow the procedure described for making the serving table shown in Plate 40 and Figure 87. For making the top of the round table shown in Figure 89, join, dowel, and glue six widths of stock. When dry, cut a 40-in. circle. Then finish all over.

2. Legs for either table are made of chromium-plated steel pipe or natural aluminum tubing, ¾ in. o.d., 12-ga. wall, and threaded at the top ends with standard ½-in. pipe threads. They are then screwed into iron sockets made up of drilled iron plates, pipe unions, and reinforcing gussets, brazed as shown. These are fastened with screws to the underside of the table and bronzed. A threaded iron pipe to be temporarily screwed into the pipe unions during the brazing, should go to the welder with a 75-deg. templet, so that each socket may be tacked at the right angle.

Metal legs are typical of the times.

Basic Table A
(SEE PLATE 41 AND FIGURES 90 AND 91)

The table shown at A in Plate 41 is an end table, straight and square in all its details. Following it are eight modifications, the front elevations of which are shown with tops. The top views are shown with tops removed. The method of construction is shown in the upper right-hand corner in Plate 41. To obtain the effect of clean structure, the wood must be well matched, and the joints tight. The finish must be excellent.

Fig. 92. End table.

More variations of the same table are shown in Plate 42. If to these were added other possible variations of length, width, and height, one can understand how free a craftsman may be when he uses the simple method of adaptation, which this plate illustrates.

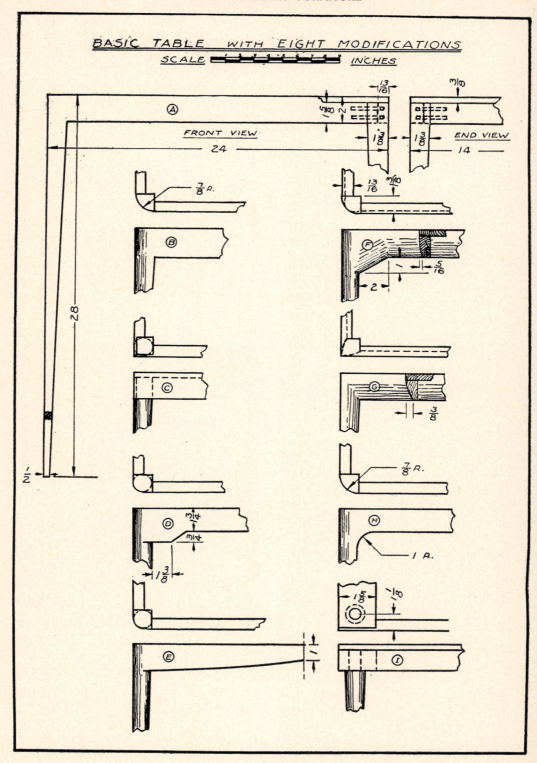

Plate 41.

The following list gives some of the measurements of useful tables:

Kind	Size of Top	Width of Rail	Dimension of Leg
Plant tables	11 × 17	1⅞	1⅜ × 1⅜
	12 × 17	same	same
Telephone table	12 × 20	same	same
Night table	14 × 20	same	same
Lamp table	12 × 23	same	same
End table	14 × 24	2	same
Tea table	14 × 27	2¼	1½ × 1½
same	15 × 26	same	same
Coffee table	16 × 28	2⅜	1⅝ × 1⅝
same	17 × 30	same	same
Serving table	17 × 36	2⅝	1¾ × 1¾
Writing table	18 × 32	2¾	same
Boy's desk	18 × 38	same	same

If the table has a drawer, add ¼ in. to all sizes and rail widths. If table is used for ordinary duty, use sizes given, otherwise add a maximum of ⅜ in. to rails and ¼ in. to legs. Table heights vary from 30 in. for the serving table, and 28 or 29 in. for writing tables, to 26 in. for end tables, and 12 to 20 in. for coffee tables.

Materials: Basswood, knotty pine, maple, beech, oak, magnolia, etc.

Stock sizes: 1½ × 1½ × 112; ⅜ × 7½ × 49; 1 × 6 × 23

Finishes: Natural, in lacquer or oil, and wax

PROCEDURE

1. Using the directions in Chapter 2, prepare the following pieces:
   1 top, ⅜ × 14 × 24, made up of two widths of stock, joined, doweled, and glued, and then planed to size
   4 legs, 1⅜ × 1⅜ × 27⅝, tapered from a point below the rail to ½ × ½ at the floor
   2 rails, 1 × 1⅝ × 21¼
   2 rails, 1 × 1⅝ × 11¼
2. Surface plane and sand all pieces.
3. Bore dowel holes into ends of rail pieces, and bore corresponding holes into legs. Follow directions given in Chapter 3.
4. Drill and countersink three screw holes into the underside of each rail piece for fastening the top. See Chapter 3.
5. Glue and clamp rails to legs. Wipe off surplus glue. Use two bar clamps on the long sides set over the center of the joint. Then, with protecting pieces under the clamps, place two other clamps over the top of the table positioned directly over joints on the short sides, gripping over the first clamps, and tighten. Pressure is directed through the sides of the latter clamps. See Figure 20.
6. Glue and screw top to table. Finish all over as directed in Chapter 4. Level the bottom and add domes to the feet.

Modifications of Table A
(SEE PLATE 41 AND FIGURES 90 AND 92)

Table B. Make the table the same as table A, except round the outer corners from the top to the floor. Do this by planing the corners after assembly, each leg being held over the bench while it is being planed and rounded.

Table C. Build this table with the rails extending to the mitered outside corners. Legs are doweled into the rails as in table A, but they are cut out 3/16 in., to fit the thin outer lap of the rail shown in Figure 21. In addition, round the legs fully below the rail. See Chapter 2. This rounding is done before assembly.

Table D. The procedure here is the

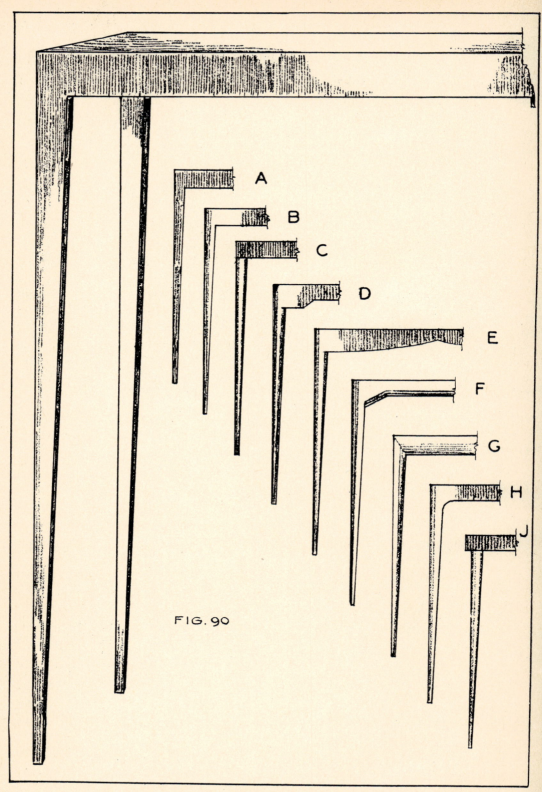

Fig. 90. Basic table and end table adaptations.

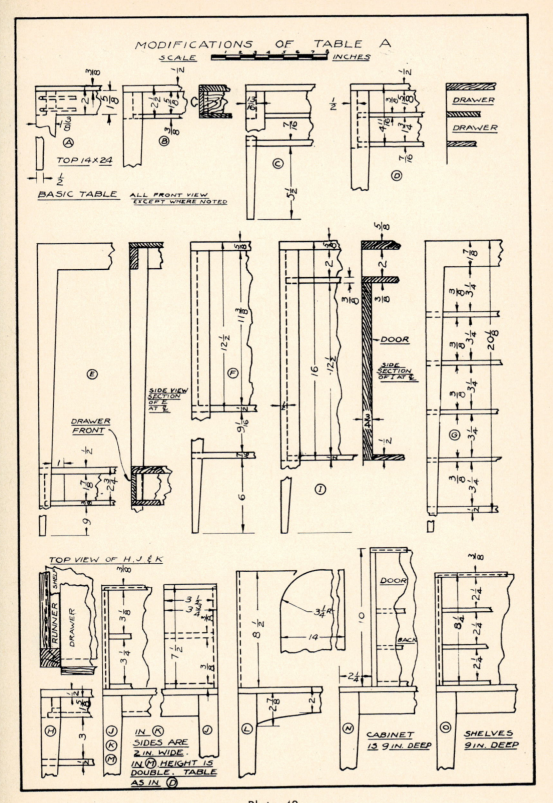

MODIFICATIONS OF TABLE A

SCALE INCHES

Plate 42.

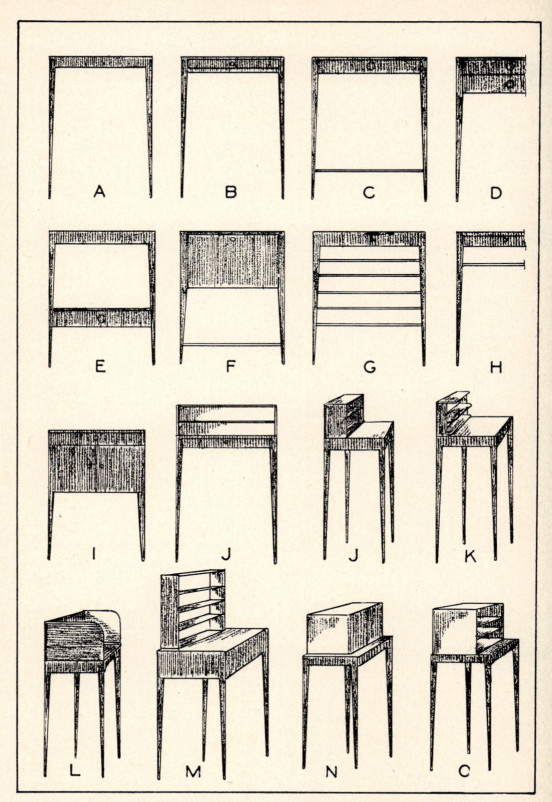

Fig. 91. Further adaptations of the basic table in Plate 41.

same as that used for table *B*. The rails are cut ¾ in. wider than those in table *B* to allow for the cutout design. Round the legs fully below the rails.

Table E. Use the dimensions of table *B*. Cut the rails to the contours shown in Plate 41. Round the legs from the rails down as in table *D*. The top is rounded into the legs, at all corners.

Table F. Use dimensions for table *B* with the exception of those for the rails which in this case are 2⅝ in. wide. Cut these to the pattern shown. After assembly, round the legs, outer corners only, and include the top. Then round each inside leg edge and the under rail edges up to a line 5/16 in. back of the outer faces, as shown in Plate 41, the rounding of each edge meeting in sharp mitered corners.

Table G. The treatment of the molded rail and leg on this table is similar to that on table *F*, the rounded legs and molded rails being cut to lines ⅜ in. back on inner leg surfaces and same on bottom rail surfaces. The leg section shown in the sketch is fairly sharp on its outer corners. The ⅜ in. dimension reduces as the taper reaches the floor.

Table H. This is table *B* with a corner piece glued oversize into each inside corner. The fillet is worked down as shown, after the glue has dried. It is then finished flush.

Table I. This table has rounded legs doweled into end blocks hidden behind the aprons, and fashioned like those in table *C*, the end blocks serving as side rails. The legs are rounded as described in Chapter 2.

Further Adaptations of the Basic Table in Plate 41

(SEE PLATES 41 AND 42 AND FIGURES 90 AND 91)

The tables described in Plate 42, and Figures 90 and 91, merely suggest some of the many that might be designed.

Table A is a basic table. Any adaptation on Plate 41 may be used as a base. Sizes may be varied at will by increasing measurements. See text for Plate 41.

Table B has an added drawer. The rail widths on three sides have been increased to 2 in. Drawer front measures $1 \times 1\frac{5}{8} \times 21\frac{1}{4}$, grooved for $\frac{3}{16} \times \frac{1}{4}$ for bottom, and rabbeted at ends $\frac{1}{2} \times \frac{1}{2}$ for sides.

Drawer sides, $\frac{1}{2} \times 1\frac{5}{8} \times 12$, grooved for bottom

Drawer back, $\frac{1}{2} \times 1\frac{1}{4} \times 20\frac{1}{4}$

Drawer bottom, $\frac{3}{16} \times 11\frac{5}{8} \times 20\frac{5}{8}$

Drawer shelf, $\frac{3}{8} \times 13\frac{3}{16} \times 22\frac{3}{8}$, cut at corners to fit around legs

The top thickness changes to ½ in.

Table C is like table *B*, with an additional lower shelf, measuring $\frac{7}{16} \times 14 \times 24$, set into leg notches.

Table D is a telephone table with two drawers like the one in table *B*, and two drawer shelves and side and rear panels.

2 side panels, $\frac{1}{2} \times 4\frac{3}{16} \times 11\frac{1}{4}$

1 rear panel, $\frac{1}{2} \times 4\frac{3}{16} \times 21\frac{1}{4}$

1 drawer shelf, $\frac{3}{8} \times 13\frac{1}{2} \times 23$, cut at corners to fit around legs

1 drawer shelf, $\frac{7}{16} \times 13\frac{1}{2} \times 23$, cut like the one in table *D*. Add ⅛ in. to all drawer stock heights for lower drawer. The table top is ½ in. thick.

Table E is a night table with low drawer. The table itself is table *A*, or one of its variations, Plate 41. The drawer is made like that for table *B*, Plate 42, except for its measurements. Make these pieces:

2 side panels, $\frac{1}{2} \times 2\frac{1}{4} \times 12\frac{1}{2}$, cut at each end to the angle of leg taper

1 rear panel, $\frac{1}{2} \times 2\frac{1}{4} \times 22\frac{1}{2}$, cut as above

1 drawer unit top, $\frac{1}{2} \times 14 \times 24$, cut at corners to fit around legs

1 bottom, $\frac{3}{8} \times 13\frac{1}{2} \times 23$, cut as above

1 drawer front, $1 \times 1\frac{7}{8} \times 20\frac{1}{2}$, cut as for table *B*, other drawer pieces to match

2 pieces, $\frac{1}{2} \times 1 \times 1\frac{7}{8}$, to fit at ends of drawer opening

Table F is a cabinet with a low shelf. The variations are:

Top, ⅝ in. thick

Legs taper from below cabinet

2 side panels, $\frac{1}{2} \times 11\frac{3}{8} \times 11\frac{1}{4}$

1 rear panel, $\frac{1}{2} \times 11\frac{3}{8} \times 21\frac{1}{4}$

1 bottom, $\frac{1}{2} \times 14 \times 24$, cut to fit around legs

1 shelf, $\frac{3}{8} \times 14 \times 24$, cut as above

2 doors, $\frac{5}{8} \times 11\frac{3}{8} \times 10\frac{5}{8}$

The shelf is notched into legs.

Table G is table A or one of its variations, Plate 41, with five additional shelves for magazines.

4 shelves, $\frac{3}{8} \times 14 \times 24$, and

1 bottom shelf, $\frac{1}{2} \times 14 \times 24$, all notched at four corners to fit around legs, and nailed from underneath, starting at the top shelf downward, the nails set at 30 deg., or less from the level of the shelf board.

Table H is a telephone table with a drawer and a shelf for a telephone book. The drawer has a metal box made of 16- or 18-ga. aluminum from 13×23-in. stock. The gauge line is 1 in. from three edges. Other variations are:

1 top, $\frac{1}{2} \times 14 \times 24$

1 drawer shelf, $\frac{3}{8} \times 13\frac{1}{2} \times 23$, set into $\frac{3}{8} \times \frac{3}{8}$ rail rabbets

2 drawer runners, $\frac{1}{2} \times \frac{3}{4} \times 11\frac{1}{4}$, nailed inside of drawer shelf as shown in detail in Plate 42.

1 drawer front, $\frac{1}{2} \times 1\frac{5}{8} \times 21\frac{1}{4}$, rabbeted $\frac{3}{32} \times \frac{3}{8}$ on two sides and bottom to fit metal drawer box

2 rails, $1 \times 1\frac{5}{8} \times 11\frac{1}{4}$, rabbeted underneath for drawer shelf, $\frac{3}{8} \times \frac{3}{8}$

1 rear rail, $1 \times 1\frac{5}{8} \times 21\frac{1}{4}$, rabbeted as above

1 book shelf, $\frac{1}{2} \times 14 \times 24$, cut to fit around legs

Legs as in table A

Table I is a record-album cabinet when made slightly deeper than table A. It has an upper drawer.

Legs are tapered from a point just below the cabinet.

1 top, $\frac{5}{8} \times 15\frac{1}{2} \times 24$, rabbeted $\frac{1}{4} \times \frac{3}{8}$ to accommodate the back

2 side panels, $\frac{1}{2} \times 12\frac{3}{4} \times 15\frac{3}{8}$

1 back panel, $\frac{3}{8} \times 15\frac{5}{8} \times 21\frac{1}{4}$

1 drawer shelf, $\frac{1}{2} \times 15\frac{1}{8} \times 23$, cut to fit legs

1 bottom, $\frac{1}{2} \times 14\frac{3}{8} \times 23$, cut to fit legs

2 doors, $\frac{3}{4} \times 10\frac{5}{8} \times 13$

1 drawer front, $1 \times 2 \times 21\frac{1}{4}$, grooved $\frac{3}{16}$ for bottom, and cut to lap sides $\frac{1}{2} \times \frac{1}{2}$

2 drawer sides, $\frac{1}{2} \times 2 \times 13\frac{1}{4}$, grooved for bottom

1 drawer back, $\frac{1}{2} \times 1\frac{1}{2} \times 20\frac{1}{4}$

1 drawer bottom, $\frac{3}{16} \times 12\frac{7}{8} \times 20\frac{5}{8}$

Table J is a variation of table A with shelves built over it.

1 shelf top, $\frac{3}{8} \times 3\frac{3}{4} \times 24$

1 each, bottom and shelf, $\frac{3}{8} \times 3\frac{1}{2} \times 23\frac{1}{4}$

2 sides, $\frac{3}{8} \times 3\frac{3}{4} \times 7\frac{1}{8}$

1 back, $\frac{1}{4} \times 7\frac{5}{16} \times 23\frac{5}{8}$

Sides and top are rabbeted $\frac{3}{16} \times \frac{1}{4}$ for back panel

Table K is similar to table J, except that the dimensions of the shelf sides are $\frac{3}{8} \times 2 \times 7\frac{1}{8}$, and shelves and top are rounded back to meet the sides.

Table L is a tea table, much like table A, except that the rails are arched from $2\frac{7}{8}$ in. wide to 2 in. Therefore, rail pieces are cut $2\frac{7}{8}$ in. wide, other sizes being like those on A. The upper box pieces are:

2 sides, $\frac{3}{8} \times 14 \times 8\frac{1}{2}$ in., rounded as shown, and rabbeted on the back edge to hold the back panel

1 back, $\frac{3}{8} \times 8\frac{1}{2} \times 23\frac{5}{8}$

Table M is table A with high shelves: the shelf pieces are:

1 top, $\frac{3}{8} \times 3\frac{3}{4} \times 24$, rabbeted for back

2 sides, $\frac{3}{8} \times 3\frac{3}{4} \times 14\frac{1}{8}$, rabbeted $\frac{3}{16} \times \frac{1}{4}$, as shown

1 bottom, $\frac{3}{8} \times 3\frac{1}{2} \times 23\frac{1}{4}$

3 shelves, $\frac{3}{8} \times 3\frac{1}{2} \times 23\frac{1}{4}$

1 back, $\frac{1}{4} \times 14\frac{5}{16} \times 23\frac{5}{8}$

Table N is table A, or one of its variations, with a cabinet above. Make cabinet pieces:

1 top, $\frac{3}{8} \times 9 \times 19\frac{1}{2}$

2 sides, $\frac{3}{8} \times 9 \times 9\frac{5}{8}$

1 bottom, $\frac{3}{8} \times 8\frac{3}{4} \times 18\frac{3}{4}$

2 shelves, $\frac{3}{8} \times 8\frac{3}{8} \times 18\frac{3}{4}$

1 back, $\frac{1}{4} \times 9^{13}\!/_{16} \times 19\frac{1}{8}$

2 doors, $\frac{3}{8} \times 9\frac{3}{8} \times 9\frac{1}{4}$

Top and sides are rabbeted $\frac{3}{16} \times \frac{1}{4}$ for back

Table O is another table like *J*, with a larger upper shelf.

1 shelf top, $\frac{3}{8} \times 9 \times 24$

2 sides, $\frac{3}{8} \times 9 \times 7\frac{7}{8}$

1 bottom, and 2 shelves, $\frac{3}{8} \times 8\frac{3}{4} \times 23\frac{1}{4}$

1 back, $\frac{1}{4} \times 8^{1}\!/_{16} \times 23\frac{5}{8}$

Top and sides are rabbeted $\frac{3}{16} \times \frac{1}{4}$ for back.